A Holy and Living Sacrifice

The Eucharist in Christian Perspective

Ernest Falardeau, S.S.S.

A Liturgical Press Book

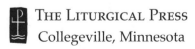
THE LITURGICAL PRESS
Collegeville, Minnesota

Cover design by David Manahan, O.S.B.
Cover art: The Last Supper, detail; fresco. St. Bernard's Church, Munich, Germany.

The Scripture quotations contained herein are from the New Revised Standard Version Bible, Catholic edition, © 1989 by the Division of Christian Education of the National Council of Churches of Christ in the USA. Used by permission. All rights reserved.

1   2   3   4   5   6   7   8

Library of Congress Cataloging-in-Publication Data
Falardeau, Ernest R.
    A holy and living sacrifice : the eucharist in Christian
  perspective / Ernest Falardeau.
        p.   cm.
    Includes bibliographical references.
    ISBN 0-8146-2329-8
    1. Lord's Supper.   2. Lord's Supper and Christian union.
  I. Title.
  BV825.2.F35   1996
  234'.163—dc20   95-20971
                                                        CIP

Contents

Preface   vii

Introduction   ix

Chapter 1   The Eucharist as Sacrifice   1

The Eucharist as Sacrifice in Scripture   1
Antecedents in the Hebrew Scriptures   1
New Testament   2
The Eucharist as Sacrifice in Theology   3
Thomas Aquinas and Sacrifice   3
The Centrality of Sacrifice   4
Denials   5
A View from the Councils   7
Sacrifice in Controversy   7
Ecumenical Insights   8
Some Important Points of Convergence   8
The Eucharist: Symbol and Reality   9
The Eucharist as Sacrifice and Spirituality   11

Chapter 2   The Eucharist "For the Forgiveness of Sins"   14

Penance and the Eucharist before Lateran IV   15
Penance and the Eucharist after Lateran IV   16
The Eucharist as Propitiation   16
The Eucharist and the Forgiveness of Sins   18
The Sense of Sin and Forgiveness   19
The Eucharist and Liberation   21

Chapter 3   The Eucharist as Memorial *(Anamnesis)*   24

Anamnesis in Agreed Statements   25
Vatican II on Liturgy   25
Implications for Spirituality   26
Anamnesis—The Ecumenical Convergence   27
The Rediscovery of *Anamnesis*   27
Biblical Background: The Jewish Passover   28
Sacrifice as *Anamnesis*   29
Eschatology   29
Memorial of What?   30
Vatican II—The Eucharistic Sacrifice   31
Memory and Spirituality   31
A Merciful God   32
Do This   32

Chapter 4   The Eucharist as Communion   35

New Testament Insights   35
    1 John 1:4-6   35
    First Corinthians   36
    The Body of Christ   37
    Ephesians 4:1-32   38
    *The Church and the Eucharis*t   39
Interreligious Dimensions   41
The Human Family   42
Eucharistic Sharing   42
Communion and Spirituality   43
Reformation Insights   44

Chapter 5   The Eucharist and Priesthood   46

Ordained Priesthood and Sacrifice   47
The Universal Priesthood of the Laity   47
Sacrament of Self-giving   48
An Antidote to Selfishness   48
Sacrifice of the Church   49
The Eucharist Makes the Church   50
Sacraments for People   51
A Love Feast in the Spirit   52
Priesthood, Clericalism, and Authority   53

The Priesthood of the Laity   54
  Participation as Essential   55
  Ordained Priesthood and Laity   56
  Priesthood and Sacrifice   56

Chapter 6   The Eucharist, the Spirit, and the Kingdom
(Eschatology)   58

The Sign of the Kingdom   58
The Orthodox Witness   59
The Holy Spirit and the Eucharist   60
The Spirit and the Liturgy   60
Epiclesis   61
Epiclesis in Ecumenical Convergence   61
The Creative Spirit   63
Eschatology   63
The Second Coming of Christ   64
Eucharist and Eschatology   65
A Monastic View   66

Chapter 7   The Eucharist and Spirituality   68

Sacrifice as Self-giving   69
Eucharistic Contemplation (Adoration)   70
Eucharistic Spirituality after Vatican II   70
Eymardian Spirituality   71
Learning from Our Ecumenical Friends   71
The Eucharist as Spirituality   72
Ecclesial Dimensions   73
Eucharist and Ecclesiology   74
A Holy and Living Sacrifice   76
Eucharistic Sharing   77

Bibliography   79

Preface

For some years I have been studying and writing about the Eucharist as sacrifice. A four-month sabbatical at the Institute for Ecumenical and Cultural Research, Collegeville, Minnesota, provided me the time and surroundings for a more extensive probing into the question. What I found is a good number of excellent works delineating the convergence and even consensus around this subject. This agreement began with the initiation of the faith and order discussions of the World Council of Churches culminating in the monumental work *Baptism, Eucharist and Ministry*.[1] Among those who contributed to this agreement are the Groupe de Dombes in France, and Orthodox, Catholic, Evangelical, and Pentecostal dialogue groups from many parts of the world.

My previous work *"One Bread and Cup: Source of Communion"*[2] brought together some of the insights of Eucharistic spirituality and contemporary ecumenical theology. This work centers on the Eucharist as sacrifice and draws from the growing convergence among Christian Churches and its implications for the spiritual life of Christians.

At the time of the Reformation, the sacrificial nature of the Eucharist was hotly debated. Even now the subject is generally avoided seemingly for ecumenical reasons. As a matter of fact the notion of sacrifice is central to Eucharistic theology. It is at the heart of the contemporary convergence.

I believe it is important to draw attention to this aspect of the ecumenical convergence and even more importantly to draw from it the consequences for spirituality today. For in the end what really matters is how Christian truth enriches the lives of men and women of our time.

Albuquerque, New Mexico
December 8, 1994

---

1. World Council of Churches, *Baptism, Eucharist and Ministry,* Faith and Order #111 (Geneva: World Council of Churches, 1982).

2. Ernest Falardeau, *One Bread and Cup: Source of Communion,* (Wilmington: Glazier, 1987, Collegeville: The Liturgical Press, 1990).

Introduction

This is a book of spiritual theology, specifically of Eucharistic spirituality. In *One Bread and Cup: Source of Communion* I did an initial investigation, leaning heavily on spiritual theology and the spirituality developed in the Congregation of the Blessed Sacrament since Vatican II.

In this volume I hope to focus more centrally on the sacrificial nature of the Eucharist. I have found exploration of this facet of the Eucharist to be of extreme importance for the theology of the Eucharist and also for the conclusions that this theology presents for Eucharistic spirituality.

There is an ecumenical value to this study. The Eucharist as sacrifice was at the epicenter of the earthquake in the sixteenth-century debates. The Reformers, beginning with Luther, denied the Catholic view on this matter. While it is true they were more disturbed by the popular view and practice of the Eucharistic piety, still they felt strongly that these practices were rooted in a false understanding of the very nature of the Eucharist, particularly in its sacrificial aspect.[1]

It is not my intention to renew the sixteenth-century debates, even though in this more ecumenical climate we can discover some merit in the underlying view of the Reformers. The Church was indeed in need of reform, and some of the critiques of the Reformers were very justified. My purpose is rather to move beyond these debates to the ecumenical consensus currently in place. Given this understanding of Eucharist, what implications can we derive for Eucharistic spirituality today?

What is the purpose of this book, then? It is two-fold. On the one hand it seeks to ground current Catholic devotion more deeply in the solid ecumenical theological consensus presently in place among the Churches. That tradition rests squarely on biblical and patristic evidence and understanding. Secondly, it seeks to explain to our ecumenical friends how such devotion is consonant with the ecumenical convergence, and how it can lead to a more fruitful living of the Gospel.

The Eucharist in Christian Perspective

What has become evident from my research is that a convergence and even a consensus has been emerging on the question of the Eucharist as sacrifice. Rather than the bone of contention it has been for hundreds of years, theologians in a wide spectrum of traditions from the Orthodox to the Evangelical and Pentecostal have come to understand that the Eucharist is the sacrifice of Jesus Christ made available through sacramental signs, for us, for our salvation and "for the forgiveness of sins."

The question may be asked: why write another work on the sacrificial aspect of the Eucharist? The first reason is the importance of this central aspect of the Eucharistic mystery. The second is because the ecumenical convergence has much to teach us about the role of the Eucharist in living the Christian life.

Unfortunately the din of controversy obscured the central truth that the Eucharist is the sacrifice of Christ made available for us and for our salvation. Important implications of this truth were lost and all traditions were thereby impoverished. But we can recover the full beauty and splendor of the Eucharist by a return to its central theme and the implications of this great mystery for Christian living.

Current ecumenical literature shows the role of the Catholic Church in preserving the sacrificial nature of the Eucharist. In bilateral and multilateral responses, Rome has consistently pointed out the neglect of this central theme. Without an understanding of the sacrificial nature of the Eucharist, a full knowledge of the Eucharist is not possible.

The World Council of Churches' Faith and Order document *Baptism, Eucharist and Ministry* (with the help of the many bilateral and multilateral efforts to reach this important convergence) has painstakingly put together an agreed statement which gives its rightful place to this aspect of the Eucharist.[2]

This book is most interested in the spiritual and dynamic consequences of the affirmation that the Eucharist is a sacrifice, Christ's, the Church's, and ours.

The value of an ecumenical approach is that it moves away from the limitations of sectarian, scholastic, and polemical issues and the repetition of old clichés and modes of exposure. To be ecumenical is to bring into focus the wide sweep of perspectives from the Orthodox emphasis on the Kingdom of God to the Pentecostal emphasis on the pneumatic and epicletic (Holy Spirit) dimensions of the Eucharist.

Protestant theology is far more concerned with what goes on in people than in what goes on in the bread and the wine. Catholic emphasis on the objective transformation of the elements (and the people) stresses that the beauty is in the object as well as in the beholder. That is, there is beyond the symbol and together with it, the reality of the presence of the Son of God among us.

My task is to bring together the fruitful theological reflections and liturgical histories which point the way to a better celebration and reception of the Eucharist.

The audience for which I am writing is a broad one. It is for all Christians: ecumenists but also for non-professional people interested in Christian unity. Christians of all ages and backgrounds who look to deepen their faith in the Eucharist and their understanding of its nature and power, I hope, will find inspiration in these pages.

Several years of reading, writing and researching the Eucharist, specifically in its sacrificial aspects, have helped me to know that the Reformers and contemporary theologians from other Churches, have something very valuable to contribute to our mutual understanding of the Eucharist. At times their contributions may seem like the mirror image of what we experience in our own lives. But, as Alice in Wonderland teaches us, even seeing imperfectly "as in a mirror" can be most revealing. The sharp contrast of reality and truth and our babbling expressions of it, particularly when the subject is the divine mysteries, humble us into admitting our poverty. And in our search for truth we need to listen to the Spirit wherever he speaks. Vatican II tells us the Spirit has spoken eloquently in Churches other than our own. We need to heed and listen.

From an ecumenical perspective, the Eucharist is the Lord's Supper given to his Church "for a remembrance of me." The Bread of Life gives life to the world. The sign of our sharing in the "cup" of the Lord Jesus, the Eucharist is Paul's "cross" put into the center and the highpoint of our lives. The sharing in the Resurrection, the gift of God's Spirit, is fellowship with the Risen Lord and the banquet prefiguring his heavenly feast.

We are saved by the sacrifice of Jesus Christ; the Eucharist is a participation in that sacrifice here and now. We are transformed by the Spirit, the love of God, and are brought in closer communion with the Father.

In this full and rich perspective of ecumenical theology, I want to look at some of the main themes and issues surrounding the Eucharist today. How is the Eucharist a sacrifice? What difference does this make for us? How can we maximize this value in a practical way? How can this enhance our prayer and our living of the Christian life?

---

1. James F. McCue, "Luther and Roman Catholics on the Sacrifice of the Mass," *Lutherans and Catholics in Dialogue, III: The Eucharist as Sacrifice*, ed. Paul C. Empie and T. Austin Murphy (Minneapolis: Augsburg, 1965) 72–73.

2. WCC *Baptism, Eucharist and Ministry*, E #5–13.

1   The Eucharist as Sacrifice

The popular view of sacrifice is something "taken away," immolated, destroyed. The sacrifices of the Old Testament come to mind. However the Epistle to the Hebrews stresses, in the sacrifice of Jesus, his gift of self in obedience to the Father's will (10:10).

For Christians the sacrifice of Jesus is the paradigm. One is too easily led astray by focusing on Old Testament sacrifices or those of other religions. The uniqueness of the sacrifice of Jesus should hold center stage for Christian reflection and theology.[1]

The Eucharist as Sacrifice in Scripture

Luther was right (as were other Reformers) in affirming that the New Testament does not call the Eucharist a sacrifice. This is the reason the Reformers felt free to deny its sacrificial nature. However it was clear to Luther, as it is to us, that the entire context of the Eucharist is clearly sacrificial. There is the clear allusion to the Mosaic sacrifice of the Exodus and the Passover: "This is the blood of the covenant. . ."(Exod 24:8). Jesus, in the recorded "words of institution" speaks of his "body broken" and "blood poured out" (Luke 26:19-20).

The Gospels recall that either the meal was a Passover Meal (the Synoptics) or that it was the time of Passover (John). The Eucharist is "the new testament." There is constant reference to the "coming of the kingdom" and with that coming, Jesus will again share this banquet. Paul recalls that it is done "in his memory" and "until he comes again."[2]

Antecedents in the Hebrew Scriptures

The words of institution that Jesus uttered at the Last Supper are a clear reference to the ancient paschal covenant made by Moses in the desert. Jesus said "This is the covenant in my blood" or "The blood of the New Covenant." The allusion is clearly to an "old testament," which as a matter of fact was in the blood of the calves sacrificed for the sealing of the covenant between God and his people after Moses had read the Ten Commandments, i.e., the Covenant which God expected his people to observe. Jesus gives a new commandment for this new covenant: "A new commandment . . . that you love one another as I have loved you" (John 13:34).

There are a number of "covenants" in the Hebrew Scriptures. But the mosaic covenant is paramount for the establishment of God's people after the exodus from Egypt. The covenant of Abraham is foundational, but the covenant of Moses creates the people which returns to the Promised Land and the fulfillment of God's promises to Abraham and Isaac and Jacob and to God's people through the prophets (Exod 3:6, 15). This is the context for the New Covenant which Christ establishes with the people of faith who are to be born from the open side of Jesus Christ on the cross of Calvary.

New Testament

In addition to the account of the Last Supper, we have a number of significant and important texts in the New Testament on our subject. Obviously the sixth chapter of St. John's Gospel comes to mind. Though some deny it refers to the Eucharist, the general consensus in Christian tradition is that at least in its final verses, the text does refer to the Eucharist.[3] Paul has much to contribute to our knowledge of the Eucharist, especially in his First Letter to the Corinthians.[4]

Chapter 10 of First Corinthians describes the one body made up of many members who are one because all share in the "one loaf" (10:16-17). In the eleventh chapter he describes the Last Supper as something that has been handed down to him. His description follows the Lucan line. It adds some significant insights into the sacrificial nature of the Eucharist, its *memorial* dimension, and the kind of "discernment" required of those who prepare to celebrate "the death of the Lord . . . until he comes" (11:26).

Hebrews, the best commentators tell us, is not about the Eucharist. But it is about the sacrifice of Jesus on Calvary and how that sacrifice touches the lives of Christians after the Resurrection and Ascension of the Lord. We will need to return to these texts. But let us cite them here as a point of reference.

The Eucharist as Sacrifice in Theology

The Eucharist is the Christian sacrifice. This fact is implied in the texts of Scripture that describe what Jesus did and the context for that action. It is the Christian Pasch,[5] the early Christians clearly understood that it fulfilled the ancient Passover and replaced it. "I will no longer eat and drink this passover . . . until I drink it in the kingdom" (Luke 22:16). Jesus said at the Last Supper. "Christ our passover has been sacrificed. . . ." (1 Cor 5:7).

Thomas Aquinas and Sacrifice

Thomas Aquinas describes sacrifice[6] as "something offered to God." He classifies it as one of the outward "acts" of the virtue of religion. Aquinas teaches that we live in God's world. He is our creator and Lord. He has a right to our worship. Aquinas balances this idea with the fact that we are God's children, and that we cannot adequately praise God, thank God, or make atonement for our sins. In Christ we are given the possibility of adequate worship and religion.

This is a notion which finds resonance in the Orthodox approach to the Eucharist. For the Orthodox there is only one world: God's. Faith is not make-believe, acting "as if." It is the light to see the world *as it is,* i.e., as God's kingdom.[7] This kingdom has already come. But it is also yet to come *(eschaton).* God's kingdom will be perfectly realized when Jesus comes in glory, assembles his people for a final time, and presents the transformed cosmos to the Father for his eternal glory.[8]

The Eucharist is the sign of God's kingdom. Through the liturgy we enter more deeply into God's kingdom. It becomes part of us and our lives, and we become more deeply part of that kingdom.[9]

For the Orthodox there is only one sacrifice: that of Jesus Christ offered in history on Calvary, offered sacramentally at the Last Supper, offered eternally in heaven (as described in the Letter to the Hebrews). Calvary was a moment in history; Jesus' eternal offering in heaven is the never-ending "moment" of eternity. (Actually time and eternity are mutually contradictory.) Between these two great events is the other moment in time when we offer the Eucharist, or rather Christ offers the Eucharist for us.[10]

We share in the saving action of Jesus. His action in history saved the world. His Eucharistic action saves us. It is one saving action with an eternal and a temporal dimension. The reason why the one action can have both eternal and sacramental components is that the one action on Calvary was that of a God-man. As man he lived in history. As God he offered (and offers) an eternal sacrifice (this is the very point of Hebrews). The heart of the sacrifice is not Jesus' immolation, but his obedience, his self-offering. This disposition remains, even though the action is over. Indeed for God the saving action endures because it has an eternal dimension.[11]

Jesus is the Lord of the universe. The Risen Lord is not bound by space and time. His humanity can touch us in our time, and his divinity can have saving power always.

We are touching the heart of the mystery of the Eucharist. While words and theological concepts help us to understand, they do not exhaust the mystery. There will always be more to understand and express. Other times and places will have other insights to share as they consider Christ inviting his people to share his feast.

As we know from the past, it was precisely a failure to discuss the matter of sacrifice on the basis of Scripture that divided Christians in the sixteenth century. A recovery of the scriptural evidence will help us better appreciate the theology of sacrifice.

The Centrality of Sacrifice

The concept of sacrifice is central to the theology of the Eucharist. While there seems to be a tendency to shy away from theological discussion about sacrifice for many practical (and ecumenical) reasons, still Kevin Stevenson[12] is right in asserting that it is central and vital to a clear theological grasp of what the Eucharist is all about.

The Early Christian tradition is so very clear on the sacrificial nature of the Eucharist that anyone who denies it has the burden of the proof. The nature of sacrifice is very clear in the Hebrew Scriptures. Someone has defined it as "acted out prayer." It is prayer in action. Praise, thanksgiving, reparation/atonement, and petition are the motives for sacrifice.

There are various kinds of sacrifice. There are offerings of wheat, grain, and wine. There are sacrifices of animals that are shared by priests and offerers. And there are holocausts which are totally consumed. The latter are the most dramatic. Though we have some difficulty in empathyzing with animal sacrifice,[13] still the concept is not beyond our grasp. Someone may wonder what inspiration such a concept can have.

Denials

One of Martin Luther's first denials was aimed at the Eucharist as sacrifice.[14] Calvin and Zwingli followed suit, as did many other Reformers. Their denial was not so much an attack against the doctrine of the Eucharist as sacrifice, as an assault against the practice of Eucharistic devotion and sacramental understanding. Though the Church officially would be hard pressed to admit to what the Reformers were accusing the Church of teaching, popular understanding and semi-official writing tended to support the Reformers' allegations.[15]

What the Reformers, especially Luther, accused the Church of teaching was the Eucharist (specifically the Mass) as a "new and distinct" sacrifice. Luther saw it as another "good work" which the people were urged to use to merit God's blessings and eternal salvation. Yet in denying the sacrificial nature of the Eucharist, the Reformers were flaunting the Tradition that clearly stressed its sacrificial nature.

Obviously the real question is not *whether* but *how*. And that is the rub. Neither side had a theology strong enough to convince the other of its point of view. Indeed while the Roman side stressed tradition and scholastic theology, the Protestant side stressed the Scriptures. Hence the added difficulty of a meeting of minds.

Many excellent works, especially in recent years, have explained in coherent systematic terms why the Eucharist is a sacrifice. Much of this work was not possible in the past. We did not have adequate scriptural insights, nor did we have an adequate theology.

Scholastic theology, especially that of St. Thomas Aquinas has much to teach us. However in the sixteenth century it was in decadence. The philosophy of the time, nominalism, seemed to say that for God "anything goes." Later Enlightenment philosophy would discard it entirely. Twentieth-century "death of God" theology did little to restore the ancient tradition.

Existentialism has given us a new lease on life. So have phenomenology and the theologies reflected in Vatican II and the postconciliar period. But the ecumenical convergence, while not without its own weaknesses, has tended to take the best of existing theologies and put them to the task of interpreting the data of Scripture.

Thus we have the best, for the moment, of what we can grasp intellectually about the Eucharist as sacrifice. I would refer the reader to such excellent treatments as those of Max Thurian, Jean Tillard, and others for a complete excursus. Perhaps the following attempt will breathe some of this insight.

The Eucharist is a sacrifice because it is the memorial *(anamnesis)* of the self-offering of Jesus Christ on Calvary. The Synoptics record that in the context of the Jewish Passover, Jesus took bread and said: "This is my body which is/will be broken for you." "This is the cup of the new covenant in my blood, which will be shed for you." "Do this in memory of me." It is done for the ransom of the many.

The intent of Jesus was definitely to leave to his followers a symbolic and fruitful sign of his self-sacrifice. Hebrews tells us that the sacrifice of Jesus on Calvary has an eternal dimension, rooted in the divinity of Christ. The risen body and blood of the Savior is a vivifying spirit. Ascended to heaven, always making invocation for us, Jesus Christ pleads to the Father for his body which is the Church. He asks that the Spirit be sent to the Church and those who receive his risen body.

Thus are achieved the forgiveness of sins (salvation), the transformation of human nature (sanctification) together with the seed of immortality for the body of those who receive. Each Christian is thus more deeply rooted in Jesus Christ. (Baptismal grace and life are nourished.) Communion with the Father in Jesus Christ and with the Son and Holy Spirit are effected. So is, and by the same token, communion among all who are united in the love of God and God's salvific and sanctifying work.

All of creation praises God through the voice of human beings who recognize God in all creatures. Sacrifice thus is a continuation of the praise and glorification of God that began silently in the love of the Trinity: Father and Son in the Holy Spirit. That love was poured out in all creation which reflects God's glory, power, and love. That love continues in his Son, Jesus Christ, the firstfruits of those to be saved.

Through Christ and in him we are brought into the love of God by the gift of the Holy Spirit. This gift of love was signified and given to us in faith and baptism. It continues and is nurtured by the Eucharist. The Eucharist, unlike baptism which is to be received only once (like birth), is to be received often because (like food) it renews, nourishes, repairs, and refreshes the Christian in his/her pilgrimage.

We will develop in separate chapters the concepts of memorial *(anamnesis)* and communion *(koinonia)*.

A View from the Councils

The Catholic emphasis on sacrifice has been widely revised since its expression in the Council of Trent.[16] Vatican II has done much to preserve Tridentine teaching, but goes far beyond it. And though this has been a minor theme in Catholic theology since the Council, it remains a rich one, a mine to be explored.[17]

Post-Tridentine and early-twentieth century Catholic theology sought to explain sacrifice in terms of immolation.[18] The sacraments "produce" what they signify. And so "in some way" Christ is "sacrificed" in the Mass. It was particularly this view that irked the Reformers. Though today we "soft-pedal" any idea of the Eucharist as a "new and different" sacrifice, both the popular perception at the time of Trent, and even the official formulation seemed to justify that interpretation.

Today in bilateral and multilateral statements, the Catholic Church makes it clear there is no new sacrifice in the Mass. The stress, rightly, is on the Eucharist as the *same* sacrifice as Calvary (the priest, the offering, the victim) are one.[19]

The Eucharist is the self-offering of Jesus Christ, our head, offered on Calvary, eternally present to the Father, sacramentally "available" to us for our salvation. Our offering is the spiritual sacrifice (1 Pet 2:5) of our daily lives. It is pleasing to God because it is offered by Christ on behalf of the entire mystical body. Thus the Eucharist makes the Church and expresses the Church's life.

Sacrifice in Controversy

The sacrificial nature of the Eucharist was at the heart of the controversy between the Reformers on the one hand and Rome on the other. Luther's problem was more with practice than with doctrine.[20] Rome, unfortunately, was more concerned with defending practice than with examining the truth put forth by the Reformers.[21]

If Christians had been more concerned about the unity of the Church throughout its history than with defending the *status quo*, perhaps Christianity would be one today. It is the over-riding sense of the scandal of division that drives the ecumenical movement.

Unfortunately our present concern for unity was not the dominant concern of the Church in the past. The way in which heterodoxy and those who dissented were handled left much to be desired. "Error has no rights" readily led to persecution rather than persuasion.[22]

This does not place the blame entirely on one side. The Reformers perhaps too easily preferred a Church of their own to a Church united but somewhat less perfect than the one they envisioned.

Luther's problem with the notion of sacrifice was the popular belief that it was a "work" which could be performed to "manipulate" God. In his early works he was satisfied with correcting the popular notion with the idea that the Lord's Supper is the self-offering of Jesus and our own. Luther found great consolation in this notion of sacrifice.[23]

Ecumenical Insights

In the last fifty years an ecumenical convergence has been emerging on the subject of baptism, Eucharist, and ministry. This convergence has been registered in the World Council Faith and Order document published in 1982.[24]

In the Eucharist section the notion of sacrifice is clearly reaffirmed. It is supported by the notion of passover memorial and communion in the Body and Blood of Jesus Christ. This convergence is possible because of the extensive renewal of Scripture, patristic, liturgical, theological, and ecumenical studies in the present and past century. Because of the synthesis which these studies have made possible, an ecumenical convergence could emerge.

My research has made it clear that there is much to be learned from the ecumenical convergence and from the various studies made by scholars of all Christian Churches and denominations.

I know that I only touch "the tip of the iceberg" in trying to reflect the many insights to be found. However, I believe it is worthwhile examining that convergence and drawing some of its implications.

Some Important Points of Convergence

The following list is not exhaustive, but suggests a few of the important points of convergence on the Eucharist:

1) The Eucharist is the same sacrifice as that offered on Calvary.
2) The Eucharist is the sacrifice of Jesus Christ.
3) The Eucharist is the offering of the sacrifice of Christ, not in its historical reality, but in its eternal dimensions.
4) The eternal sacrifice of Jesus Christ contains the self-sacrificing obedience offered on Calvary.
5) The Eucharist is the self-offering of the whole Church, the body of Christ, head and members.
6) The Eucharist does not "add" anything to the sacrifice of Jesus Christ, as though it were not sufficient in itself.
7) The Eucharist is the same priest, victim, offering as that offered on Calvary.
8) The Eucharist is not a "pure memory," it is rather an *"anamnesis,"* i.e., a memorial by which those remembering/celebrating today share in the saving power of the past event.
9) The essence of what Jesus offered on Calvary was self-sacrificing obedience.
10) The essence of what Christians offer are their own self-offering and obedience.
11) The key words for a Christian understanding of Eucharist are: memorial, communion, *epiclesis,* meal of the kingdom, and sacrifice of praise and thanksgiving.

The Eucharist: Symbol and Reality

William Crockett in *Eucharist: Symbol of Transformation*[25] describes the development of Eucharistic theology in terms of symbol and reality. He underscores the unity between symbol and reality in the apostolic and patristic periods of Christian history.

Indeed until the twelfth century the world view of the Church was essentially Platonic and Augustinian. Thomas Aquinas was able to reinterpret the patristic view in Aristotelian terms. He was always careful to keep the balance between symbol and reality and frequently cited Augustine as the authority for his teaching.[26]

However with the decline in scholastic theology in the late Middle Ages and the introduction of nominalist philosophy the stage was set for the Reformation. Both sides lacked appropriate "tools" to speak to each other. Luther emphasized Scripture. Trent went back to Thomas

Aquinas and scholastic terminology (unfortunately sometimes through his later interpreters). Calvin was perhaps best qualified for the moment with his knowledge of the Fathers and his keen philosophical bent of mind.

The struggle, as Crockett describes it, was essentially a matter of shifting views of the world. In the Platonic view the visible world was but a shadow of ultimate and divine reality. The real was more real than the visible.

In the Aristotelian view, the visible world was real, but underneath it—so far as understanding is concerned—is the metaphysical world. For Aristotle and Thomas metaphysics was more important than physics (or cosmology). Indeed though their cosmology and physics have long been discarded by the scientific world, their metaphysics continues to be the basis for sound theological discourse today.[27]

With the coming of the Reformation, the Enlightenment, and the modern scientific age, we have lost the sense of symbol. For moderns there seems to be a necessity to choose between symbol and reality. In the world of religious values and theology, symbol and reality are not diametrically opposed, they are inter-related.

This is particularly true when we are speaking of sacraments, which are a very special kind of reality and symbol. The sacraments have never been so well defined as by Augustine. A sacrament is a visible sign of invisible grace. Indeed throughout the struggle of the Reformation, we can see the various protagonists struggling with the interpretation of symbol and reality.

Is the Eucharist (are the bread and wine) mere symbols of the reality (grace) that God wishes to give? While there were constant efforts by one side to accuse the other of distorting the matter by a selection of one element over the other, it seems to me that all were affirming that beyond the symbol there is God and the reality of grace. But how to bring these two realities together is the problem that never seems to go away.

As we rediscover the role of ritual as efficacious symbols and means of grace (whatever may be our hermeneutic), we continue to affirm, if we are men and women of faith, that "the symbol works." God gives grace and signifies his love in Jesus Christ by offering us "for our salvation" the sacred signs by which Jesus continues to save God's people in the Church.

The Eucharist as Sacrifice and Spirituality

The celebration of the Eucharist has been traditionally the center of each Christian's life. Vatican II explicitly recalls this truth.[28] For many, daily Eucharist is a pattern of life. This practice has been encouraged at least for priests and religious for many centuries. The laity, especially in the light of Vatican Council II, have also been encouraged to make the Eucharist the center of each day.

This liturgical moment focuses our lives, our ministry, our activities. Sharing deeply in the paschal mystery of Jesus Christ through the Eucharist we grow to understand how Jesus is the "way." And our lives are patterned on his cross, so that we can hope to share in the glory of the Resurrection. The joy of our lives stems from the sure knowledge that the cross leads to the empty tomb.

Patterned on the cross of Jesus, our lives have deep meaning. While we already live in peace and share the joy of the resurrection, we recognize that the glory is "not yet." We have yet a long road to walk, carrying our cross, before we reach Calvary and the glory of Easter. This paschal dimension of the mystery becomes the pattern of our lives and reveals its deepest meaning.

In Eucharistic contemplation we penetrate the mystery to find its meaning in the celebration, the proclamation of the Word and communion with Christ, the Bread of Life. Given the gift of the Holy Spirit by the Risen Lord, we learn to call God "Father" and to become sons and daughters in Jesus Christ.

Thus the celebration of the Eucharist becomes the center of our prayer, and the pattern of our living. We try to put on the "mind of Christ" and his life. Thus we realize St. Paul's ambition to "put on Christ." "For me to live is Christ" (Phil 1:21).

---

1. Xavier Léon-Dufour, *Sharing the Eucharistic Bread: The Witness of the New Testament,* trans. Matthew J. O'Connell (New York: Paulist, 1987) 283–89.

2. *Ibid.*, 203–29.

3. *Ibid.*, 248–77.

4. Hans Conzelmann, *1 Corinthians: A Commentary on the First Epistle to the Corinthians,* trans. James W. Leitch, bibliography and references James

W. Kunkly, ed. George W. MacRae (Philadelphia: Fortress, 1975) esp. 175–204.

5. Jean-Marie-Roger Tillard, *The Eucharist: Pasch of God's People* (Staten Island: Alba House, 1966).

6. Thomas Aquinas, *Summa Theologiae*, II–II, q.81–100.

7. Alexander Schemann, *The Eucharist: Sacrament of the Kingdom*, trans. Paul Kachur (Crestwood, N.Y.: St. Vladimir's, 1987).

8. *Ibid.*, 27.

9. *Ibid.*, 47–48.

10. *Ibid.*, 200–01.

11. Robert C. Crocken, *Luther's First Front: The Eucharist as Sacrifice* (Ottawa: University of Ottawa Press, 1990) 127–28.

12. Kevin Stevenson, *Accept This Offering: The Eucharist as Sacrifice Today* (Collegeville: The Liturgical Press, 1989) viii.

13. Michael Ramsey, *The Christian Concept of Sacrifice* (Fairacres, Oxford: SLG Press, 1974) 1. Ramsey says his teacher, Edward Clement Hoskyns, suggested that it would be uniquely helpful to gather all theology undergraduates studying sacrifice on a hot summer's day and let them experience the goring of a bull. There would be nothing more "experiential" to give them a feel for what the ancients did when they sacrificed.

14. R. Crocken, *Luther's First Front*, 17.

15. *Ibid.*, 84.

16. David N. Power, *The Sacrifice We Offer: The Tridentine Dogma and Its Reinterpretation* (New York: Crossroad, 1987).

17. R. Crocken, *Luther's First Front*, 148.

18. Michael G. Witczak, *The Language of Eucharistic Sacrifice:* Immolare *and* Immolatio *in Prefaces of the Roman Tradition,*(Thesis ad Lauream #118) (Rome: Pontif. Athanaeum Anselmianum, 1987).

19. ARCIC. *The Final Report,* North American Edition, (Washington: United States Catholic Conference, 1982) #5.

20. R. Croken, *Luther's First Front,* 80. I am very indebted to this excellent analysis of Luther's writings about the Eucharist as sacrifice. Luther's earlier writings are less polemical both towards Rome and later towards the other Reformers. It is particularly in these earlier writings of Luther that one finds excellent passages on Communion and how the Eucharist deepens our communion with Christ and with the entire Mystical Body.

21. James F. McCue, "Luther and Roman Catholicism on the Sacrifice of the Mass" in *Lutherans and Catholics in Dialogue III. The Eucharist as Sacrifice,* 73.

22. For a final solution to this problem in Vatican II see Donald Pelotte, *John Courtney Murray Theologian in Conflict* (New York: Paulist, 1975).

23. Martin Luther, (WA 6,369; LW 35,99) quoted by R. Crocken, *Luther's First Front,* 21.

24. WCC. *Baptism, Eucharist and Ministry,* F&O #111 (Geneva: World Council of Churches, 1982).

25. William R. Crockett, *Eucharist: Symbol of Transformation* (New York: Pueblo, 1989).

26. M.-D. Chenu, *Introduction à l'étude de St. Thomas* (Paris: 1950).

27. Edward Schillebeeckx, *The Eucharist,* trans. N. D. Smith (New York: Sheed and Ward, 1968).

28. Vatican II, *Sacrosanctum Concilium,* #10.

2

The Eucharist "For the Forgiveness of Sins"

The centerpoint of Eucharistic controversy in the West is the notion of propitiatory sacrifice. Admittedly the expression "for the forgiveness of sins" is in all the Gospel accounts of the institution of the Eucharist by Jesus on the night before he died.

The Catholic Church continues to stress the propitiatory dimension of the Eucharist. No longer to sustain a system of Mass offerings and chantry (Mass Foundations), but simply to affirm the consoling truth that a sinful people is graced by God's forgiveness each time it "remembers the death of the Lord, until he comes."

For a thousand years the Eucharist was clearly seen as the sacrament in which the faithful received the forgiveness of their sins.[1] The sacrament of penance was a rare occasion, at least in the early Church. Pastor Hermas[2] speaks of it as the "second plank of salvation." It was administered publicly by the bishop, usually on Holy Thursday, and was especially used by those guilty of apostasy, murder, and adultery.

The rite of penance for lesser offenses was introduced very gradually. The Irish monks moved to the continent around the sixth century and began to encourage its use. (It was an outgrowth of the monastic practice of the *coulpe*, confessing minor infractions of the rule to the abbot.) At first the hierarchy considered this rite of penance an abuse. It included absolution before satisfaction was made, whereas in the ancient practice one did penance before receiving absolution.[3]

At the millennium, and for a considerable time thereafter, both public and private penance were in use. Penitentials (books of guidance to confessors) indicate when each was appropriate as well as suitable penances to be made.[4]

Some Eastern rites for Penance are taken verbatim from the text of the Eucharist. (Those over fifty still remember the use of the *confiteor* and "absolution prayers" which were used both in the confessional and for the distribution of Communion outside the normal time within the Mass.)[5]

This attitude toward Eucharist and penance was largely changed in the late Middle Ages, particularly in the Fourth Lateran Council and its famous *Omnis utriusque sexus* (canon 21)[6] determination that every Christian must receive penance and Eucharist at Easter time under pain of excommunication and refusal of Christian burial.

In the mind of most people this decree established that one could not receive Communion without first going to confession. This attitude prevailed almost until Vatican II. The understanding that minor sins can be forgiven in other ways has contributed greatly to more frequent reception of Communion in recent years. At the same time it has contributed to the decrease of use of the sacrament of reconciliation.

Penance and the Eucharist before Lateran IV

It is very difficult to judge the impact of canon 21 of the Fourth Lateran Council. But at the very least, it crystalized the relationship between penance and Eucharist for many generations to come.

The rite of the sacrament of penance began as a public rite celebrated before the bishop as a remedy for "capital sins" of apostasy, murder, and adultery. The sacrament followed a time of considerable penance. Gradually, through the influence of the monks, a private rite was introduced for more common sins, with absolution being given before penance was performed.

Private penance at first was considered an abuse. Gradually the hierarchy saw the value of private confession and began to encourage it. The rule of thumb, reflected in the penitentials, was that public sin should be confessed in public penance and private sins should be confessed in private confession.[7]

Before the development of private confession, the Eucharist was seen as the normal way one obtained forgiveness of sins. (Obviously good works, especially alms to the poor and fasting were always seen as satisfaction for sin). Both sacramental and other "works" did not "buy" forgiveness. God gave it graciously in view of the saving actions of Jesus Christ. The cross of Christ is the sign of our salvation.

Because the Eucharist was so closely linked to the cross, the passover of the Lord, it is easy to understand how the Eucharist was seen as the sign and symbol of God's forgiveness of sins. The liturgical evidence of this understanding is now readily available. Unfortunately it was not equally available to both sides at the time of the Reformation. This would have perhaps prevented the Reformers from seeing penance as a human creation, rather than one of the seven great sacramental symbols of Jesus Christ for his Church.

Penance and the Eucharist after Lateran IV

What seems clear today is that at least in the popular mind, there was an absolute connection between penance and the Eucharist. The Council of Trent simply repeated Fourth Lateran in the requirement that anyone who is guilty of serious sin must confess before approaching the altar. Exception is made for the celebrant who must celebrate the Eucharist, but he is required to confess as soon as possible (CCL #916). The Jansenist influence, especially in France, is responsible for deepening this idea that one is not worthy of approaching the altar without previously preparing one's soul, particularly by approaching the sacrament of penance.

The skittishness recently demonstrated by some members of the hierarchy about the large numbers of those who go to Communion reflects earlier concerns. The idea of "unworthiness" was propagated not only by Jansenism (which accounts for much of Western reluctance to receive the Eucharist before this century) but also by many other errors and popular beliefs, some originating in rather high places.

The Eucharist as Propitiation

The Eucharist, because it shares in the sacrifice of Jesus Christ is propitiatory in nature. That is, it is "for the forgiveness of sins."

Forgiveness is something that God generously gives to those who repent of their sins. While the Catholic Church sees an important link between the sacrament of reconciliation and the forgiveness of sins, this link is dependent upon genuine contrition. Without contrition there can be no forgiveness.

For many centuries forgiveness of sins as a sacrament was clearly linked to baptism. The sacrament of reconciliation was generally linked to public penance with solemn reconciliation through the ministry of the bishop. During these centuries of practice, the Eucharist was the usual way of forgiveness. In the high Middle Ages, especially through the Fourth Council of the Lateran (A.D. 1215) the link between penance and Eucharist became more closely focused.

With the growing understanding of the Eucharist as a "dramatic sacrifice" and penance as the normal means of sacramental forgiveness of sins, some of the importance of the propitiatory nature of the Eucharist was lost. Significantly the idea of the Eucharist as propitiatory was focused more on the dead than the living. This is particularly true of Masses offered for the dead and the focus on Purgatory.

The doctrine of purgatory and indulgences was sufficiently clarified in Vatican II to need no repetition here. The idea is that every sin brings with it the need for satisfaction. Clearly there are many who have not done satisfaction for their sins during their life. The Catholic Church has taught mercifully that there is still an opportunity to expiate such a lack after death in Purgatory. However the most important "expiation" for sin is the death of Jesus Christ on Calvary.

The teaching on Purgatory was the basis for the whole system of Mass offerings, chantries, etc. which dominated the scene shortly before the Reformation. The preaching of indulgences, especially the plenary indulgence granted for contributions to the building of St. Peter's was the center of the storm for Luther and the Reformers. While this teaching continues to be an ecumenical problem, Rome's reform in Vatican II has given some hope of final resolution.

Luther perceived Catholics as saying the Mass had a value for forgiving sin for the living and the dead in a "magical" way *(ex opere operato)*. Each Mass was a new and distinct "sacrifice." It could plead for God as a "good work" and thus obtain results.[8]

Mass foundations (chantries) were established by the wealthy for the purpose of pleading their case long after they were dead. The system of Mass offerings (stipends) was implicated in this way of acting.[9]

Luther wanted to move away from this "private and silent Mass" to a celebration more centered on participation and communion. (Vatican II introduced many of his desired reforms: Communion from the cup, vernacular language, participation, prayers recited audibly, etc.)[10]

Though Luther did not deny the sacrificial nature of the Eucharist, he stressed that it was a sacrifice of praise and thanksgiving. The "propitiatory" dimension of the Eucharist, particularly as this affects the dead (and the living) was problematic for him.[11] Luther admitted that "for the forgiveness of sins" was clearly in the words of institution. He was disturbed that the proclamation of these words was made silently in the Mass of his time. The sacrificial context is clear from the New Testament accounts of the institution and the apostolic reflection on the gift given.[12]

Calvin moved further away from the sacrificial notion of the Eucharist stressing the importance of the inner workings of grace in the hearts of Christians.[13] Calvin was deeply interested in the spiritual development of the faithful. He agreed with Luther that the Mass had become too much a drama, rather than a spiritual feast. He wanted a weekly celebration of the Eucharist, but he had to settle for a quarterly Eucharist in the Reformed Church of his time.

Calvin's emphasis was on the Eucharist as "praise and thanksgiving" and as a communion "in the spirit" with Jesus, our Savior. He did not find the Catholic emphasis on transubstantiation particularly helpful. It drew too much attention to the species of bread. Like Luther he favored the use of the cup because of its rich symbolism. Inspiration was the center of his reforming message. Through the work of the Spirit, the saving action of the Risen Lord continues in his Church.

Zwingli denied the sacrificial nature of the Eucharist all together. The sacrament was the "moment of grace" for Zwingli. But not in Calvin's sense of inspiring the Christian, but in the Evangelical Protestant sense that sacraments speak to us of God's love and prepare us to receive it.[14]

The Eucharist and the Forgiveness of Sins

The importance of this subject, that the Eucharist is the ordinary remedy for our daily sins is significant. The Council of Trent explicitly stated this truth.[15] Unfortunately the message did not get through. Not only would it dissipate certain false notions about so-called "worthiness" when approaching the Eucharist,[16] but hopefully could lay to rest certain fears about Eucharistic sharing among Orthodox, Catholics, and some Protestants.

More importantly we need to correct both the Protestant view that the Eucharist has *no* propitiatory value, and the mere repetition of Trent that it does,[17] without explaining further what that means. The Orthodox perception of the Eucharist for the forgiveness of sins may be helpful here. The central idea of the Orthodox is that the Eucharist and the sacrifice of Jesus are one and the same; they are identical. As soon as one tries to bring in differences, one gets into trouble.

Westerners tend to view the Eucharist "upside down." Rather than consider the Eucharist from our point of view, the Orthodox consider it from God's point of view. God wants us to share the salvation won by Jesus Christ. The means for us to do so is the Eucharist. Rather than emphasize our doing something for God in the Eucharist, the Orthodox emphasize God doing something for us, namely, giving us a share in the sacrifice of Jesus Christ.

In this view what Jesus offers eternally before the Father is the very sacrifice offered on Calvary (Heb 10:12-15). What persists in this offering is the disposition of Jesus, his "obedience." What we offer is our sharing in his life, attitudes, and ministry. Christ offered his sacrifice as head, now we offer it as his body. He offers it for us, he makes us sharers in his self-offering. As Luther put it, we offer ourselves, giving thanks and praise to the Father for all his many blessings in Jesus Christ.

> That is, we lay ourselves on Christ by a firm faith in his testament and do not otherwise appear before God with our prayer, praise and sacrifice except through Christ and his mediation. Nor do we doubt that Christ is our priest or minister in heaven before God. Such faith, truly, brings it to pass that Christ takes up our cause, presents us and our prayer of praise, and also offers himself for us in heaven. If the mass were so understood and for this reason called a sacrifice, it would be well. [18]

The Sense of Sin and Forgiveness

For Christians this doctrine of the forgiveness of sins is very significant and very consoling. Many lament the loss of a sense of sin today. People are aware of sin. They see it every day. Indeed sin has become more widespread, more violent, more pervasive, more publicized than ever.

But sin is not easily understood theologically. To understand sin as God understands it, one needs faith. One's world view must go beyond observable phenomena. To one who lacks faith sin is just a matter of the daily news. "What can be done about it?. . . ." is a common reaction to violent crime in the streets and against strangers. Sin is a fact of life. Theologically, sin is an insult to God. It is idolatry. It is a practical denial that God is Lord. It is disobedience. Something of this magnitude cannot be atoned or even forgiven without some divine intervention (Ps 51).

This is the Christian understanding of Christ's atonement and his sacrificial offering "for the forgiveness of sins." It is not as though we were placating an angry and jealous God. Rather seeing God as Father, we recognize that his love is infinite and so found a way to satisfy justice and mercy together. He sent his Son that we might have forgiveness, grace, and life.

Prodigal sons and daughters, we recognize our misery, but the Father "goes out before us" to welcome us home in forgiveness and rehabilitation (Luke 15:11-32). Our elder brother, far from scolding the Father for his mercy, accepts to be part of his plan of redemption and offers to become "one like us except for sin" (Heb 4:15) so that he may lay down his life for us sinners.

The modern problem is not with sin; it is with forgiveness. Men and women are in deep depression over their inability to conquer addiction and abuse. Hope comes to them when they can recognize a force and power greater than themselves. This power is divine—the loving God and Father of our Lord Jesus Christ.

I am particularly moved by the plight of persons with addictions who come repeatedly to the sacrament of reconciliation for the peace and strength they need to continue to struggle for improvement. Often they wonder whether they should refrain from Communion because of their sins or approach Communion because of their need. I believe they should find the answer in the Gospel. Jesus ate and drank with sinners. He did not turn them away from his table. Neither should we.

I am not suggesting we should condone sin. I am suggesting we should practice mercy. For a thousand years the Church developed two rites of penance, one public and one private. In the meantime the Eucharist was considered the ordinary and normal remedy for sin. Based on that understanding I suggest the Church needs to implement the mandate of Vatican II and develop both public and private reconciliation and thus meet the need of the faithful.

It is not the role of the Church to separate sheep and goat at the altar rail. Christ welcomed all. While heeding the Apostle's advice "let each one examine himself" (1 Cor 11:28) and the liturgical rite that we ask forgiveness (especially from each other for lack of love) we then proceed to offer our gift of self and receive the gift of Christ giving himself to us.

The Eucharist and Liberation

Jon Sobrino in an article on our subject[19] recalls the implications which this topic brings to mind. Sin is more than individual. It is structural as well. In fact liberation theologians would like much more emphasis on structural sin and corporate injustice than is presently being given.

Much of the crime and violence in the world is being driven by the injustice of our capitalist system. The law of supply and demand and free market economies does have limitations and a flip-side. Pollution of the environment, exploitation of the poor and working classes, extremes of wealth and poverty, failure of governments to meet the needs of the masses are some of the more glaring examples of structural sin in our culture.

The Eucharist has a role to play in this context. The Eucharist recalls the Gospel. It is the gift of the Holy Spirit who can attune our hearts and minds to recognize such sin in our lives.

Gustavo Gutiérrez has something to say on this subject as well.

> Without a real commitment against exploitation and alienation and for a society of solidarity and justice, the Eucharistic celebration is an empty action, lacking any genuine endorsement by those who participate in it. . . . "To make a remembrance" of Christ is more than the performance of an act of worship, it is to accept living under the sign of the cross, and in hope of the resurrection. It is to accept the meaning of a life that was given over to death—at the hands of the powerful of this world—for love of others.[20]

In essence, he is saying we cannot receive the Eucharist without "putting on the mind of Christ," without becoming sensitive to the needs of the poor and the social injustice in our world. Through the

Eucharist we are united to Christ and to our brothers and sisters. Whatever we do to the least of these, we do to Christ in whom we have life.

1. Jean-Marie-Roger Tillard, "The Bread and Cup of Reconciliation" in *Sacramental Reconciliation*, ed. Edward Schillebeeckx, Concilium #61 (New York: Herder and Herder, 1971) 38–54.

2. *Pastor Hermas* Mand.4,3,6. Rouet de Journel #7. This passage indicates that Penance is available once after baptism.

3. José Ramos-Regidor, "Reconciliation in the Primitive Church and its Lessons for Theology and Pastoral Practice Today" in *Sacramental Reconciliation*, 76–88.

4. B. Poschmann, *Penance and the Anointing of the Sick,* trans. F. Courtney. New York: 1964. See also L. Bieler "Penitentials" in *New Catholic Encyclopedia* (New York: McGraw-Hill, 1967) vol. 11, 86–87.

5. Franz Nikolasch, "The Sacrament of Penance: Learning from the East" in *Sacramental Reconciliation*, 65–75.

6. *Omnis utriusque sexus fidelis, postquam ad annos discretionis pervenerit, omnia sua solus peccata saltem semel in anno fideliter confiteatur proprio sacerdoti, et iniunctam sibi paenitentiam pro viribus studeat adimplere, suscipiens reverenter ad minus in Pascha Eucharistiae sacramentum, nisi forte de consilio proprii sacerdotis ob aliquam rationabilem causam ad tempus ab eius perceptione duxerit abstinendum; alioquin et vivens ab ingressu ecclesiae arceatur et moriens christiana careat sepultura. Unde hoc salutare statutum frequenter in ecclesiis publicetur, ne quisquam ignorantiae caecitate velamen excusationis assumat. Si quis autem alieno sacerdoti voluerit iusta de causa sua confiteri peccata, licentiam prius postulet et obtineat a proprio sacerdote, cum aliter ille ipsum non possit absolvere vel ligare* ([Canon 21] Fourth Lateran Council DS 812).

7. B. Poschmann, *op. cit.*

8. Robert C. Crocken, *Luther's First Front: The Eucharist as Sacrifice* (Ottawa: University of Ottawa Press, 1990) 80.

9. B. J. Kidd, *The Later Medieval Doctrine of the Eucharistic Sacrifice* (London: SPCK 1958) 26–31.

10. Vatican II, *Sacrosanctum Concilium,* esp. #11.

11. Martin Luther (WA 6,358; LW 35,85) quoted by R. Crocken, *Luther's First Front,* 18.

12. R. Crocken, *Luther's First Front,* 126.

13. W. Crockett, *Eucharist: Symbol of Transformation,* esp. 148–60.

14. W. Crockett, *Eucharist: Symbol of Transformation,* 138–48.

15. This sacrament is also to be a remedy to free us from our daily de-

fects and to keep us from mortal sin. It was Christ's will, moreover, that this sacrament be a pledge of our future glory and our everlasting happiness and, likewise, a symbol of that one body of which he is the head (see 1 Cor 11:3; Eph 5:23). He willed that we, as members of this body, should be united to it by firm bonds of faith, hope, and love, so that we might all say the same thing, and that there might be no dissensions among us (see 1 Cor 1:10). Council of Trent, Sess. XIII, cap. 2 DB 1638, TCT 720.

16. St. Peter Julian Eymard had to fight the Jansenism of his time on this subject. He left the Congregation of the Blessed Sacrament with a tradition stressing that reception of the Eucharist is based on human need, not on worthiness.

This tradition helps us today to understand new situations of human need such as people with addictions, divorced and remarried, interchurch families, people from other Christian Churches requesting the Eucharist for legitimate spiritual benefit, etc. Such human situations need to be reevaluated today in the light of his principle.

17. Council of Trent, Sess. XXII, cap. 2 DB 1743 and can. 3 DB 1753.

18. Martin Luther, WA 6,369; LW 35,99. quoted by R. Crocken, *Luther's First Front,* 20–21.

19. Jon Sobrino, "Liberation from Sin" in *Theology Digest* 37 (1990) 141–45.

20. Gustavo Gutiérrez, *The Theology of Liberation* (Maryknoll: Orbis, 1973) 262–63 [quoted by Horton R. Davies, *Bread of Life and Cup of Joy: Newer Ecumenical Perspectives on the Eucharist* (Grand Rapids: Eerdmans, 1993) 218–19.

3   The Eucharist as Memorial
(Anamnesis)

To fully understand the concept of memorial one must return to the biblical setting of the term. Jesus indicates that the Eucharist is to be celebrated "in memory of me." The New Testament, especially John, tells us that the setting was the Passover.

Whether or not Jesus ate the "seder" continues to be discussed. It is certain that Jesus wanted his disciples to understand what he was doing by a reference to the Paschal meal. This is the context repeated by Mark-Matthew and Luke-First Corinthians. In the Jewish view the Passover is not merely a remembrance of the past. One celebrates the Passover in order to become one with the people who were liberated, and thus share their liberation.[1]

Leo the Great in his homilies uses the term "celebration" with the poignant meaning of memorial.[2] To celebrate is to share in the mystery we remember. Orthodox perceptions of the Eucharist are comprehensive. We remember not only the moment of Calvary, but also the incarnation, the life at Nazareth, the public life with its preaching and miracles. We remember the controversies, the growing hostility, the arrest, agony in the garden, the betrayal, the crucifixion, the burial and the empty tomb and the resurrection. We remember finally the ascension and glorification of Jesus and the sacrifice he presents eternally to the Father. This is the mystery of Christ. And this mystery we remember, we celebrate, we proclaim.[3]

Cardinal Ratzinger in a homily for a feast of Mary, recalls that "she remembered these things, pondering them in her heart" means that Mary became fertile ground for God's Word, but she added her own experience of life. Similarly we must remember in a way that involves more than memory. It must involve our entire person and spiritual energy. More than recall, we participate in the mind and spirit of Jesus. We have communion in his mystery. We share with our lives the mind and heart of Christ. Thus he penetrates our life, and we are joined to his.

Animals, we are told, remember. But it is simple recall. A person remembers in a unique way. It is a curse or a blessing that he or she can recall yesterday's pain and can anticipate tomorrow's. He or she can bridge past, present, and future. This kind of memory is at work.

But there is a deeper theological notion involved. Memorial in Christian theology shares the rich overtones of the memorial celebrated by Moses as he led the people out of slavery into the promised land. Jesus refers to that context by the use of the term "new covenant" and by alluding to the pouring out of blood in the Mosaic covenant. The bread is broken and the blood is "poured out" for the remission of sins, i.e., for the liberation of Christians from the bondage of sin and the kingdom of Satan.

Anamnesis in Agreed Statements

Current agreed statements are careful to point out that *anamnesis* is not mere remembering. It is a representation. In some real though mysterious way, the sacrifice of Jesus on Calvary is made present for Christians today.[4] It is the one and same sacrifice of Jesus that is now *sacramentally* made present so that Christians may share the saving grace and fruits of the sacrifice of Christ.

There is something very *real* about the reenactment of Jesus' self-giving. But reenactment does not mean a repetition today of the bloody event of the past. This idea of duplication was at the heart of the controversy between Lutherans and the Catholic party.

Vatican II on Liturgy

Vatican II in its decree on liturgy departs from the dichotomy of Trent. Trent used two sessions for the Eucharist and entitled them: *de sacramento Eucharistiae* and *de Sacrificio Eucharistiae*. Theology since the Middle Ages made the same distinction between sacrament and sacrifice. But Vatican II uses the term (for the first time) *Eucharistic sacrifice*.

The theology of the past stressed a representation of the sacrifice of Calvary, and theologians were at a loss to explain how such a representation could be "unbloody." Their explanations were not entirely satisfactory. Thanks to reformation reaction and further ecumenical exploration, Vatican II was able to bring the dichotomy which divided Trent and the Reformation into a new ecumenical synthesis. The Eucharist is a "Eucharistic sacrifice"—a sacrifice of praise and thanksgiving. This is its predominant theme. This is not to deny its propitiatory value. But that value lies in its link with Calvary. As a ritualization of a saving historical event, the Eucharist now enters a new category.[5] The Eucharist does not replay the historic event, it rather celebrates, memorializes, and makes present its eternal dimension, its salvific dimension "for us."

Vatican II has sent us back to our Jewish roots to find the meaning of the Last Supper in the context of the Passover which Jesus celebrated with his disciples. Without this biblical and liturgical understanding we can go around in circles theologically without adequately explaining the core of truth about the Eucharist as sacrifice.

Implications for Spirituality

Nor is this truth without value to us spiritually. Life and worship are intended, in Vatican II's view, to find a new synthesis in our day. Unfortunately this spiritual synthesis is something many continue to long for, without sensing they have achieved it—at least fully.

The Liturgy needs to be more than a quiet moment when everything stops so that we might pray. Vatican II suggests it must be the summit and source of our spiritual life. It is the apex at which life and worship meet, "God and we at table are sat down." Time and eternity, sin and grace, Jesus and the Christian come together. It is a time of refreshment and renewal. But it is a time of offering as well. Christ the head offers himself and he offers us, as we offer ourselves. We remember, we celebrate, we believe. Our faith is now actualized. It goes beyond the truth we profess, to become a light by which we see the kingdom promised and achieved sacramentally.

The late Middle Ages failed to grasp the depth of scholastic theology. It was unable to see the faith of Thomas in his teaching. Beyond the words of theology there is faith seeking understanding. The articulation of faith and the search for understanding must always continue.

The celebration of the liturgy is the moment when we profess our faith: "Christ has died, Christ is risen, Christ will come again." We renew our faith as well, by receiving the Spirit given by the Risen Lord as first fruits of his saving action. This epicletic dimension of the Eucharist, emphasized by the East and underestimated by the West, is something we need to rediscover as we celebrate the paschal mystery in the Eucharist.

To remember liturgically is to become pregnant with grace and the mystery of Christ and to give birth to Christ in our lives. To remember is to share the mystery, take it into our flesh as the Word became flesh for our sakes. It is to be absorbed in the Spirit and filled with his gifts. Born again not just once, or by an emotional experience, the Eucharist makes us born again daily with the outpouring of the Spirit and our response, as Mary's: "Let it be done to me as you say. I am the Lord's servant."

Anamnesis—The Ecumenical Convergence

Though the ecumenical convergence reflected in BEM and ARCIC's *Final Report* agrees on a certain understanding of *anamnesis*, this is not to imply that there are not other understandings.[6] However this view, expressed in the agreed statements, is at least a common ground where all can find an understanding of the Eucharist that brings together all of the elements that need to be brought into a synthesis for our time.

Further development of the convergence is possible and will be useful. Faith constantly seeks greater understanding, and God's revelation of himself continues in history as we move forward on our pilgrim way.

There are those who might want anamnesis to be more real, and others who want it to be more symbolic. The one wanting the sacrament to be more "productive," causal, or active. The other wanting it to be more a "sign" of God's grace and activity than man's.[7] The current view is a *via media* and will require some dialogue and effort to find universal acceptance.

The Rediscovery of *Anamnesis*

The current ecumenical convergence has rediscovered the meaning and importance of the biblical concept of memorial *(anamnesis)*.

Because this concept was not fully understood at the time of the Reformation, both the Catholic and the Protestant side were unable to fully explain how the Eucharist can be at one and the same time a memorial of Calvary and a present offering.

The Catholic side stressed the link between Calvary and the Eucharist. The Protestant side stressed the link between the Eucharist and the eternal offering of Jesus in heaven. Today we realize that the Eucharist is both and more. Though we can never fully exhaust the mystery and our efforts to understand it in faith, still we have much more understanding today, as a result of a better grasp of how the Eucharist is a memorial of the passion, death, and glorification of Jesus.

Biblical Background: The Jewish Passover

The Eucharist was instituted in a Passover setting. At least the Gospel writers thought it important to recall that the Passover was near (John) and that Jesus was eating the Passover with his disciples (Luke).

Scripture scholars continue to debate whether or not Jesus celebrated the Passover. The problem is not that the Gospels try to say otherwise, but the need to synchronize the chronology of the final days of Jesus. This question need not concern us here. What matters for us is that the Gospel writers tell the story of the institution of the Eucharist entirely in the context of a Passover "seder."

There are constant references to the "covenant" with words taken verbatim from the covenant that Moses made with God's people after God's revelation on Sinai.

Theologians are agreed that to understand the Eucharist, one must understand the concept of memorial as it exists in the Jewish Passover. The text of Exodus is clear.[8] Those who celebrate the Passover are to consider that what happened to the people of old, now happens to them. The deliverance from the slavery of Egypt is enjoyed by all who celebrate the Passover in freedom today.

Similarly, we who celebrate the Eucharist enjoy the liberation, salvation and redemption merited by Jesus on Calvary. *Anamnesis* is more than remembering. It is sharing through memory. And the power to share is not of human making, but divine. Jesus gave us a way to share the victory of his cross. We share that victory in different ways through each of the sacraments. But we share it in a magnificent way through the Eucharist which is both sacrifice and sacrament.

Sacrifice as *Anamnesis*

The Eucharist is sacrifice as *anamnesis*. There are many kinds of sacrifice—holocaust, sin offering, thanksgiving, etc., and there are different ways in which one can offer sacrifice. The Eucharist shares the nature of thanksgiving offering. And it does so much in the way that Passover is a thanksgiving offering for the liberation of God's people from the slavery of Egypt.

The Catholic Church in its long tradition has stressed the link between the Eucharist and Calvary. The Church stresses the propitiatory nature of the Eucharist. Vatican II does not deny that tradition. It simply emphasizes that what dominates in present understanding of the Eucharist is its "Eucharistic" element.

We give thanks to God for the gift of salvation in Jesus Christ. The "price" of that salvation is the precious blood poured out and the body broken on the cross. Rather than emphasize the justice of an "angry God," the cross of Christ helps us to understand the depths of the love of Christ for us and of God's love for us. "God so loved the world . . . ." (John 13:13).

Eschatology[9]

While we stress the link between the Eucharist and Calvary, it is even more important to stress its link with the eternal sacrifice of Jesus. Hebrews tells us that Jesus is forever offering his self-offering of Calvary. Indeed the entire mystery of Jesus is self-giving. It was the obedience of Jesus that merited our salvation.

God is self-giving.[10] In the Trinity the Father shares his life with the Son, and they share their love with the Holy Spirit and vice versa. The purpose of the incarnation is to "reveal" the infinite love and self-giving of God. And so Jesus gave himself in obedience at the very first moment of his earthly existence: "Behold I come to do your will, O Lord" (Heb 10:7). This earthly self-offering mirrors the eternal self-offering of the Son.

The Book of Revelation speaks of the Lamb who was slain, but underscores the eternal dimension of his sacrifice. The Orthodox view of things underscores this eternal and eschatological dimension of the Eucharist. We are dealing here with a mystery, but one that has eternal dimensions. Rather than looking back at Calvary, which obviously is important, present understanding of the Eucharist urges us to look forward to the *eschaton* and the eternal sacrifice which Jesus offers on our behalf.

Mark Santer[11] stresses self-offering in the Church's sacrifice. The Eucharist is the symbol of God's self-offering, the gift of himself, revealed by Jesus Christ. Christ in turn offers himself to the Father on Calvary and in the Eucharist. We need to respond to God's self-offering by the gift of ourselves.

He points out that this self-offering is required as we hear the Word proclaimed, as we offer our gifts of bread and wine, as we repeat the actions and words of Jesus at the Last Supper, as we commune with him in Eucharistic Communion, and as we live our Christian lives. We must become what we offer, we must become the body of Christ, living out in our daily actions the forgiveness, healing, care, and concern of Jesus for those around him.

Memorial of What?

Thus we should be able to grasp that the Eucharist is a memorial in many senses. It is a remembrance of God's eternal activity "before the world began," the act of creation (symbolized by fruit of the earth and the vine; work of human hands) and the long history of salvation from Adam and Noah, Moses and King David, to Jesus and the Apostles, and gifts given in our lives and our time. The *mirabilia Dei* are what we remember and give thanks in Christ and with him and through him to the Father, Son, and Spirit.

We remember the future, when Christ will come again in glory to gather his elect. Those who have believed and hoped in him will be gathered as his sheep and welcomed into the Father's house forever (Matt 25:34-40).

What we offer to God is the sacrifice of Jesus Christ. Rather Jesus, who offers his sacrifice forever before the throne of his Father, makes it possible for us to enter into his offering, his prayer, his thanksgiving and praise. His atonement becomes ours, and in sign and symbol we are given a foretaste of heaven.

The Kingdom of God that will be presented by Jesus to the Father at the end of time is the kingdom we work and sacrifice to build. That kingdom will come whether or not we do anything to bring it about. But the glory of that kingdom will be both God's work and our own. Our call is to share the creative work of the Creator, the redemptive work of the Son, and the inspirational and sanctifying work of the Spirit. All of this reality is summarized and has its source in the Eucharist, which is God with us (Emmanuel), and our communion with God.

Vatican II—The Eucharistic Sacrifice

Vatican II stresses that the Eucharist is a thanksgiving sacrifice. This shift of language is not so much a concession to ecumenical concerns as an expression of what is at the very heart of the Eucharist. The clearly more ecumenical expression is a realization that the focus of the Church at Eucharist is on thanksgiving and praise for God's marvelous love and kindness.

The Jewish concept of *berakah* comes to mind in this context. Every Jewish prayer, every sacrifice ultimately can be reduced to an expression of thanks and praise to God for his goodness, justice and mercy. Because the Eucharist is steeped so deeply in Jewish tradition, it shares in this praise-thanksgiving nature. While there is no denying the propitiatory nature of the Eucharist, still it is even more important to stress its *"eucharistic"* nature.

Memory and Spirituality

A study of memory in human anthropology would be significant for a complete grasp of *anamnesis*. Much work has been done in the area of psychology concerning the healing of memories. Morton Kelsey's work[12] on the importance of dreams in therapy comes to mind as well.

Human beings have a distinct kind of memory. Though animals have sense memory, and this faculty is acute in primates and other animals, it is not the vivid power to recall in detail the events of the past. Only in humans is this power united with will and intelligence making it a very important human capacity.

In the spiritual life memory plays an important role. This can readily be seen in terms of remembering God's blessings, mighty works, and the personal and collective sinfulness of human beings. Memory should be an important part of wisdom. Many a philosopher has pointed out that if we forget the mistakes and sins of the past, we are condemned to repeat them.[13]

In the Eucharist we particularly remember God's blessings, mercy, and our need for forgiveness. Moreover memory plays a salutary role in praise and thanksgiving as well as reparation and atonement. Petition is more a recalling of our needs than a need to tell them to God. He knows all things, our needs as well.

When God forgives, we are told by the Scriptures, he casts our sins as far as "east from west" (Ps 103:12). He no longer remembers our sins. If we remember them, it should be in gratitude for God's forgiveness, rather than an unwillingness to forgive ourselves. God's mercy endures. It heals. It binds up our wounds and leads us to hope for a better response to grace in the future.

A Merciful God

Too often popular piety dwells morbidly upon failings. This can only have the effect of discouragement. The Scriptures remind us of our frail humanity and encourage us to cast our troubles on the Lord, "for he is merciful" (Exod 34:6).

This dimension of God's love needs to be more evident in the way we speak about the Eucharist. As we have stressed in an earlier chapter, the Eucharist is given for the forgiveness of sins. This forgiveness needs to play an important role in our efforts to put sin behind us, and to move forward with hope toward the eternal kingdom and our share in the heavenly banquet.

Memory serves an important function in our *living out* the Eucharistic Communion. As we receive Jesus who loved the poor, the sinner, the marginalized, we must put on his mind. We must put on Christ, so that our actions are filled with loving self-giving to those most in need of our help and God's love.

Do This

We do more than remember the words and actions of Jesus. We need to imitate those actions, especially the service he gave his disciples at the Last Supper. John does not repeat the words of institution. He recalls the actions of Jesus. The towel and the basin are also "Eucharistic symbols." They remind us that having communed with Christ, we need to serve him in our brothers and sisters.

What we do is more than repeat words. We repeat actions—living actions, so that our sacrifice may be a "living sacrifice." The relationship between Eucharist and life is a real one.

If the Eucharist is the sacrifice of the whole Christ, it is our self-giving united to that of Jesus, our head. If the Eucharist is life-giving and Spirit-filled, it is our service of others and our recognition that they are Christ-bearers and filled with the same Spirit who is the bond of peace. We form one body with those who eat the one loaf. We form one family with all those who share our humanity and for whom Christ died.

The emphasis is on action, not ritual. The words of Jesus that we remember are part of the prophetic tradition. Best expressed by the Suffering Servant Songs, this tradition emphasizes that the time for ritual sacrifice is ended. A new covenant has been instituted by Christ, a covenant in his blood, in his self-giving. And our sharing in that mission of salvation will require that we lay down our lives in the service "of the many" (Mark 10:45).

Sin is forgetting God. Grace is remembering him.[14] In the Eucharist we remember, we recall, we enter into God's view of the world and offer praise and thanksgiving, reparation and prayer in and through Jesus Christ, our high priest.[15]

---

1. Xavier Léon-Dufour, *Sharing the Eucharistic Bread: The Witness of the New Testament,* trans. Matthew J. O'Connell (New York: Paulist, 1987) 102–16.

2. St. Leo the Great, *Sermo 6 in Nativitate Domini,* 2–5.

3. The Orthodox liturgical formulas, especially in the anaphora, stress the total mystery of Christ. The WCC Lima Liturgy reflects this view that the Eucharist remembers the entire life/mystery of Christ.

4. World Council of Churches, *Baptism, Eucharist and Ministry,* #5.

5. Salvatore Marsili, "The Mass, paschal mystery and mystery of the Church" in *The Liturgy of Vatican II: A symposium in two volumes,* ed. William Barauna, Peritus of the Council, English ed. Jovian Lang (Chicago: Franciscan Herald, 1966) 2:4–5.

In a long footnote the author points out the differences between Trent and Vatican II on the Eucharist.

6. David Gregg, *Anamnesis in the Eucharist,* Grove Liturgical Study #5 (Bramcotte Notts, England: Grove, 1976).

7. *Ibid.*

8. Exodus 12:25-27.

9. I will develop some of these ideas in chapter 6. Here and later I am indebted to the insights of Geoffrey Wainwright and his classic text, *The Eucharist and Eschatology* (New York: Oxford University Press, 1981).

10. James F. White, *Sacraments as God's Self Giving: Sacramental Practice and Faith* (Nashville: Abingdon, 1983).

11. Mark Santer, *The Church's Sacrifice* (Fairacres, Oxford, England: SGL Press, 1975).

12. Morton T. Kelsey, *Dreams: A Way To Listen To God* (New York: Paulist, 1978).

13. Santayana among others comes to mind.

14. A. Schmemann, *The Eucharist: Sacrament of the Kingdom,* trans. Paul Kachur (Crestwood, N.Y., St. Vladimir's, 1987) 126.

15. *Ibid.,* 129–30.

4   The Eucharist as Communion

The concept of communion *(koinonia)* is richly described in the New Testament. It has become a key focus for the ecumenical movement today.[1] Communion is at the heart of the Eucharist.[2] One can never exhaust this rich topic.

New Testament Insights

Communion is well described in the New Testament, particularly in the classic text of 1 John 1:4-6. Paul in 1 Corinthians 10:16-17; and chapters 12–14 gives further reflection (this theme is taken up again in Romans 12).

1 John 1:4-6

Christians are in communion with Christ and through him are in communion with God (Father, Son, and Holy Spirit). Because we are in communion with God in Christ, we are in communion with one another. Communion is the goal of Christian evangelization and catechesis.

The paradigm for Christian unity is the Triune God. God is perfectly one, yet three divine persons. Each person has a distinct identity and relationship to the other. Love, freedom, and shared life characterize the life of God and the life of the Christian.

John 6 makes it clear the purpose of Christ's coming, of his sacrifice, and of the Eucharist is to share the life of the Father. The Bread of Life gives us a deeper share in the life of Christ, as Christ shares the life of the Father, so shall we if we have faith and share the Eucharist.

The life of Jesus is shared through baptism, and it is nourished through the Eucharist. Communion is at the heart of the Eucharistic mystery.[3] The purpose of the Eucharist is not simply a momentary emotion, however noble and lasting. Its purpose is radically deeper, namely a share in divine life. That life begun at baptism by our incorporation into the Risen Lord is nurtured by the ebb and flow of Christian living. The summit and source of this tide of life is the Eucharist.

The Reformers drew the attention of the Church back to Communion. The Eucharist had become a "drama" to be watched, rather than a life to be lived. By focusing anew on Communion, the Reformers hoped to bring about a revitalization of Christians. Unfortunately they did not completely succeed, largely because they were unable to break through the barriers long standing against frequent Communion in the Church.

First Corinthians[4]

The context that Paul establishes for writing this letter is the disunity existing in the Christian community. The existing factions lead people to choose sides and to proclaim the origin of their baptism and catechesis: "I am for Paul, I am for Cephas, I am for Apollos" (1 Cor 1:12).

Paul puts in a disclaimer: "I baptized very few people. None of you were baptized by me" (1 Cor 1:14). And what difference would that make? We all belong to Christ.

After discussing various causes of division among the Corinthians (one of them being an infamous case of incest), Paul then touches on the notion of sacrifice and how sharing in the sacrifice of idols makes one a "member" thereof. He exclaims: "You cannot be members of Christ and members of idols. The cup we drink and the bread we break make us members of Christ" (1 Cor 10:14-21).

"Because the bread is one, we though many, become one bread, because we share the one loaf" (1 Cor 10:17). "The cup of blessing we share is a communion in the blood of Christ" (1 Cor 10:16). This Eucharistic doctrine is at the heart of Christian understanding of the Eucharist. Augustine, Thomas, and Vatican II all proclaim the same truth.

At the end of First Corinthians, chapter 11, Paul makes the point clear: if you do not discern the Body of Christ in the Eucharist, you really are not celebrating the Lord's Supper at all (11:20 and 29). The entire context of First Corinthians is unity among Christians. Though the highpoint of Paul's teaching is in the tenth chapter, the theme runs throughout. It is taken up again in the twelfth chapter where Paul develops the meaning of membership in the body of Christ.

The purpose of the Eucharist is to unite Christians. If the Eucharist becomes a bone of contention, a focus of strife, it is defeating its purpose, or rather Christians are not using it (celebrating it) as they ought.

The abuse Paul describes makes the Eucharist a countersign. The rich and the poor are divided by their wealth and their food. The one eat and drink to excess, while the others go hungry. The synaxis which should bring them together, leaves them farther apart. Instead of the forgiveness of sins, the Eucharist only achieves the condemnation of those who eat and drink unworthily. And the unworthiness is not simply the sinfulness of Christians, but their failure to recognize the Lord in their brothers and sisters—a sign they have failed to recognize him in the breaking of bread.

The Body of Christ

The twelfth chapter of First Corinthians develops the image of the body of Christ of which Christians are members. Paul stresses the sharing of gifts for the good of all the Church. This idea is repeated in the twelfth chapter of the Letter to the Romans.

First Corinthians 12 and Romans 12 develop a similar theme: you are the body of Christ. The purpose of diversity in the body of Christ is the good of the whole. As in the human body, each member is important to the good health of the entire body, so the gifts and ministries of each Christian contribute to the building up of the Church.

One of the clear results of sin is individualism. The rugged individualist is the icon of American and modern culture. We built a nation and a world on the idea that to be truly human is to be able to "go it alone." And thus we are "people of the lie."[5] For by nature we are social animals. We are dependent upon others from birth to the grave. Parents, family, friends are all necessary not merely for a better life *(bene esse)* but for very existence. The self-made man (or woman) is a poor architect. We bear in our bodies, in our bones, the influence of generations before us (it is in the genes). Parents and siblings, friends and peers have all contributed to who we are.

But in the Christian view of things, we do not exist for ourselves, but for God. It is God's world. We are not the "be all" of it, but a very tiny part. And we are created to give as well as receive. The Eucharist is a constant reminder of the self-giving of Jesus Christ.[6] It is a call for our self-giving to others. A consciousness that we are the body of Christ, that we are the extension in time and history of what he was at the beginning, the revelation of God's self-giving. He gave his life as a proof that "greater love than this no one has. . . ." (John 15:13).

At the heart of the Christian view of things is the *kenosis* of Jesus Christ. Though he was God, he did not cling to that dignity, but humbled himself, even to death on a cross (Phil 2:5-8). His *kenosis* (emptying out of himself) was the cause of his glory and our salvation.

To celebrate the Eucharist is to renew our covenant with God that we will live the Christ-life. We will put on the mind and actions of Christ. We will not live for ourselves, but for others, as Jesus did. The Eucharistic sacrifice is both a recalling and a celebration of life as self-giving. "It is more blessed to give than to receive" (Acts 20:35). "Greater love than this, no one has, that one lay down one's life for the life of one's friends" (John 15:13).

Ephesians 4:1-32

One Lord, one faith, one baptism. . . Rather than a minimum statement of what unites Christians could we not see Ephesians as the *satis est* of the Augsburg Confession. If we can agree on this much, need we ask more? Historically more was required. But not as much as either side, Catholic and Protestant, required of each other since the Reformation. The differences among Christians in the post-apostolic Church were fundamental. They were concerned with Trinitarian and Christological accuracy. But what divides Christians today is far more in the area of theology and "theologoumena." They are not in the area of creed or gospel faith.[7]

Dialogue has brought us a greater realization of the faith we hold in common. Our differences have been revealed as "not church dividing." We really should be one Church; indeed we are one Church. But we need to acknowledge our unity.

Ephesians is a statement which helps us to focus on the essentials of our unity: one Lord, faith, baptism, Father, goal, life. The Eucharist unites us in the prayer of Jesus for the unity of all who believe in him. It unites us in his eternal offering to the Father for the salvation of all. In a similar vein the Letter to the Ephesians stresses how one faith, one baptism makes us one in the Lord and in our relation to one God and Father. All of these Pauline texts deserve frequent reflection. They are at the heart of biblical inspiration to work for unity.

The essential communion that Christians have with Christ and through him with the Trinity is the basis for all other considerations of communion *(koinonia)*. By baptism we are incorporated into Christ and life in God, in the Spirit. Through this incorporation into Christ, the head, we are members of the Church, the body of Christ. The Eucharist is the nourishment, the growth and development of this life in Christ, in the Spirit, in God and in the Church.

Jesus was particularly concerned with sinners and with the poor. Our incorporation into Christ moves us into a life of grace and therefore away from sin. Our incorporation into Christ, who had God's own love for the poor, the marginalized, those who suffer, makes us aware of our need to "put on Christ" and to have his heart and attitude toward our brothers and sisters who are ill, poor, and marginalized. This concern should characterize the Church as an institution. The "high and mighty" are not in the Church to serve themselves but to serve one and all, with a predilection for the poor (understood as all who are in need). We have touched on this aspect of the Eucharist as we described social sin. These realities touch the core of the Eucharist as we consider communion.

The Church and the Eucharist

Of all the concepts in theology the most important is communion *(koinonia)*. This is true especially for ecclesiology but equally for the Eucharist. This central idea was particularly helpful to the Church for an explanation of how it viewed other communions. While "sister-church" was useful, particularly in describing the relationship between the Orthodox Church and the Catholic Church, the real breakthrough came when Vatican II was able to say of the Churches of the Reformation that they are *"in real though imperfect communion"* with the Church of Rome.

The foundation for Christian communion lies in baptism. Baptism in Christ establishes the basis for all communion. John's First Letter explains this "fellowship" very clearly. Fellowship with Jesus

Christ is the basis for Christian "fellowship" with the Father and the Spirit as well as among Christians. The end of the Eucharist is to deepen this fellowship (cf. John 6). It is the means by which Christians are united with Jesus in his passion and resurrection.

Vatican II explains the "communion/*koinonia*" which exists between the Church of Rome and other Christian Churches in the following degrees.

The Orthodox (Ancient Eastern and Eastern Orthodox) are considered to be in *"almost full communion"* with Rome. The reason is because the Eastern Churches have not changed either their doctrine or practice since the beginning. They have preserved the apostolic succession of bishops, the "catholic" tradition of faith, and the discipline of the ancient Church. They are called sister-churches in Vatican II, a status they have enjoyed from the very beginning.

Protestant Churches of the West are said to be *"in real though imperfect communion."* This means there is a communion among all the members of these Churches and the Church of Rome. It is real—not just symbolic. It is imperfect because there are major doctrinal issues that have not been resolved by the Churches. This imperfect communion can be perfected. Indeed it can become "full communion" through dialogue and *rapprochement.*

The Anglican Communion is said to have "a special place" in this schema of relationships.[8] This is because the Anglican Church believes the historic episcopate must be preserved, and the Church is therefore hierarchically constituted. Leo XIII in *Apostolicae Curae* declared Anglican Orders to be invalid. This presents Rome and Canterbury with an unresolved problem.

In addition to this question of apostolic succession, there is also the question of doctrine. Under Henry VIII (and Cranmer) and other monarchs (Edward, Elizabeth I, Charles II), a number of Protestant positions were adopted by the Anglican Communion. These were recorded historically in the Thirty-nine Articles which continue to influence the faith of Christians in this communion.

ARCIC. *The Final Report* has done much to bring Catholic and Anglican positions, particularly on Eucharist, Orders, and authority, (including papal authority) closer together. Other points, e.g., salvation and communion have been treated in the agreed statements of ARCIC II. The international commission has been recently reorganized and continues its important dialogue. Among the questions before this commission are ethical questions, Anglican Orders, and women's ordination.

The World Council of Churches, especially through its Faith and Order Commission, has done much to move all of the Churches closer together. Its monumental work *Baptism, Eucharist and Ministry* has been widely disseminated and discussed. It is having a genuine impact on the Churches and their efforts to move toward visible unity and communion. The theme of the 1993 International Faith and Order Conference (the first since Montreal in 1963) held at Santiago de Compostella, Spain, discussed *Toward Koinonia/Communion in Faith, Life and Worship* setting the stage for progress into the Third Millennium.

The task for the Churches at this time (and the people within them) is to "receive" the insights of the ecumenical world. Through baptism, we are indeed one. We share a communion in Christ with the Three Persons of the Trinity and with all other Christians living and dead. We must acknowledge and give visible expression to this reality.

The World Council of Churches suggests sharing of the Eucharist. Orthodox, Catholic, and Evangelical and Pentecostal Christians have problems with Eucharistic sharing at this time. Further progress in doctrine and faith are needed before the Eucharist can be a legitimate, valid, and fruitful sign of the communion that is ours. If Eucharistic sharing is limited at this time, it will nevertheless continue to be both a goal and a means to deeper communion among all Christians and all Churches.

Interreligious Dimensions

Though our communion grounded in baptism and Eucharist is obviously more "ontological" with regards to other Christians, it is also connected to those of other faiths. Jesus came to save all. Vatican II tells us that the Spirit moves in other Churches. It also affirms that Christ saves people of faith in other religious traditions.[9] This is particularly true of Judaism, since God's covenants are never revoked. God's promises of salvation remain for the people of the original covenant.[10]

Our desire to bring about God's kingdom needs to find concrete expression in cooperation with all those who share religious values and understand that the world is God's creation, and we are its stewards. Similarly our concern and cooperation extends to those who do not believe. Not only do we pray for them in the most solemn liturgy of Good Friday, we also seek to work with them for the betterment of all that is human in our world.

The Human Family

At the core of our faith and the Hebrew Scriptures is the fact that God is the Creator of all. In this view of the world, every human being is part of the human family and the family of God. In this context all that is human is precious in our eyes because it is precious in the eyes of God our Father. Every human being is filled with divine existence. We are all destined to share the family banquet with all the saints. The Eucharist is a foretaste of the heavenly banquet to which all are invited.

Our hope for "realized eschatology," i.e., the Kingdom of God reflected in the world around us, rests in our knowledge that we are stewards of God's creation. As such we cooperate with all men and women of good will, who seek to better the world in which we live. God's glory is the ultimate goal of all that exists.

Our Eucharistic celebration praises and thanks God for the marvels of his creation, of redemption, of sanctification and glorification. The Eucharist is also the source of our spiritual energy to continue our efforts for the coming of God's kingdom in our world, as a reflection of God's kingdom to come in full glory.

Eucharistic Sharing

All those who seek the unity of the Church see a compelling reason to hasten the day when all will be able to share in the Eucharist. It is the goal of the ecumenical movement. And this is not simply because it will be a symbolic gesture of the unity achieved. It is because the essence of the Church is a people gathered to share Communion in the Lord.

As long as the reality signified by the sign is a broken reality, a Church divided, the Eucharist is not fully all it ought to be. The problem is not simply the brokenness of the Church. It is the inauthenticity of the Eucharist. The bread should be a sign of the communion of all who are one in baptism and faith in Christ. If there are Christians who are one in faith and baptism and who cannot share in one bread, then there is something wrong with the Church and the Eucharist.

Augustine saw it very well. So did the early Fathers. Indeed the Orthodox liturgy put it well when it dismissed all who were not to receive the Eucharist. Being present after this point indicated one's desire to receive Communion.[11]

Theologians and liturgists have been pointing out the implications of communion for social outreach. But we cannot fully grasp the social imperative of the Eucharist until we have fully understood its theological implications. Our efforts to work together for a better world need to grow out of our awareness of our communion in the Body of Christ. "No one hates his own body" (Eph 5:29). If we are conscious of the body of Christ, we will be conscious of our need to love and assist other members of that body.

Communion and Spirituality

For St. Peter Julian Eymard the very heart of the Eucharistic mystery is Communion. In his long retreat at Rome (1865) he reflected upon the mission of the congregation he founded. He realized that what he had put in the constitutions of the Blessed Sacrament Fathers and Brothers spoke too much of an external decorum. There was not a sufficient emphasis on the interior service, the self-giving which should characterize those who live by the Eucharist. In reflecting on this deficiency he wrote that the heart of the matter is communion with Christ. The hours of prayer before the exposed Eucharist are simply to deepen the communion with Christ which we share through baptism.

Our communion with Christ is what makes the Christian life real. It is the fruit of the Eucharistic sacrifice and the goal of the Christian life ("For me to live is Christ" [Phil 1:21]). But Christ can fill our lives only if we empty them of all selfishness, sinfulness, and ourselves. As much as possible he must be the center of our life and our thoughts. His mind and attitude should characterize our thoughts and actions (Phil 2:5).

As Vatican II put it, the Eucharist is the source and summit of the Christian life.[12] It is the source of our apostolic activities and the place where we surrender to Christ ourselves and our actions so that he may offer them to the Father who gives us his Spirit and his life in ever greater measure.

Reformation Insights

In focusing on communion, Luther wanted to bring the Church back to its original view of the Eucharist. Unfortunately the people were not ready to move into frequent reception of the Eucharist. At best the Reformers were able to introduce a monthly celebration of the Eucharist and perhaps a quarterly reception of Communion.

However, the return to the realization that the Eucharist was essentially a sacred meal or banquet was an important development. This clear understanding of the Eucharist was far closer to the ancient Church's view of the Eucharist. Apostolic times were more colored by the eschatological dimensions of the Eucharist, i.e., that it was a foretaste of the banquet of heaven. But the correlation between the banquet of the Eucharist and the banquet of heaven was clear and unmistakable.

With the Medieval emphasis on the Eucharist as "drama" and re-enactment of Calvary, a very important dimension of the Eucharist was lost.

---

1. World Council of Churches, Faith and Order Conference, Santiago de Compostella (Spain) August 1993 *Toward Koinonia in Faith, Life and Witness.* The revised Faith and Order Discussion Paper (under the same title) can be found in *Ecumenical Trends* 22 (June 1993) 2/82–24/104.

2. Ernest Falardeau, *One Bread and Cup: Source of Communion* (Wilmington: Glazier, 1987. Collegeville: The Liturgical Press, 1990).

3. Thomas Robert Artz, *One in the Body of Christ: Robert Isaac Wilberforce and the Theology of Concorporation* (Ann Arbor: University Microfilms International, 1985).

4. Among the Commentaries on First Corinthians, we suggest: Hans Conzelmann, *Commentary on the First Epistle to the Corinthians,* trans. James W. Leitch, bibliography and references James W. Dunkly, ed. George W. MacRae, (Philadelphia: Fortress, 1975).

5. M. Scott Peck, *People of the Lie: the Hope For Healing Human Evil* (New York: Simon and Schuster, 1983).

6. James F. White, *Sacraments as God's Self Giving: Sacramental Practice and Faith* (Nashville: Abingdon, 1983).

7. Lutherans and Catholics in Dialogue III, *The Eucharist As Sacrifice,* 24.

8. "Among those (communions) in which Catholic traditions and institutions in part continue to exist, the Anglican communion occupies a special place" (Vatican II, *Unitatis Redintegratio,* #13).

9. Vatican II, *Nostra Aetate,* #1.

10. Vatican II, *Nostra Aetate,* #4.

11. Alexander Schmemann, *The Eucharist: Sacrament of the Kingdom,* trans. Paul Kachur (Crestwood, N.Y.: St. Vladimir's, 1987) 88.

12. Vatican II, *Sacrosanctum Concilium,* #10.

5   The Eucharist and Priesthood

"You are a chosen race, a royal priesthood, a holy nation, a people set apart. . . ." (1 Pet 2:9). Vatican II rediscovered the priesthood of the laity and reaffirmed the role of the laity in the Church and in worship.

The clericalization of the Church continues to be a problem. Gradually the laity will find its rightful place in the Church and in liturgy. Meanwhile reflection on the universal priesthood of the laity will help clarify the underlying theology and spirituality. This is particularly true for Eucharistic theology.

The only priest in Christianity is Jesus Christ. He is priest by nature as well as by vocation. He is the one and only mediator between God and creation. "According to the line of Melchisedeck" as we read in Hebrews (referring to Genesis and Psalm 2).[1]

Every other priesthood, ordained and unordained, shares in the priesthood of Jesus Christ. Through baptism we become members of Jesus Christ, the eternal high priest. We become "a holy people, a priestly people, . . . to offer spiritual sacrifices pleasing to God" (1 Pet 2:9). The spiritual sacrifices we offer, together with Christ our head, are our obedience to God's will and the works that flow from that obedience.

The sacrifice of Jesus Christ is his self-offering, his obedience to the will of the Father. Walking in his footsteps, Christians "put on the mind of Christ" (Phil 2:5) and offer their gift of self, their obedience, and the works that flow from them.

The priesthood of the laity becomes especially active and vibrant in the offering of the Eucharist. Rather than spectators at a "drama" enacted by an ordained minister, the faithful are active participants, priests of the New Testament—the new order—who offer with Christ through the sacramentality of the ordained priesthood.

Ordained Priesthood and Sacrifice

Ordained priesthood shares in the priesthood of Christ. The priest acts "in persona Christi." He represents Christ as an icon. He speaks in his name and opens the book of the Word and offers the bread of life and the cup of salvation. Ordained priesthood and lay priesthood are complementary. They are not in competition. Each has its function in the Church. The one serves the other. Indeed ordained ministry is especially patterned after the service of Christ (cf., John 13:12-17).

Ordained priesthood is the service of leadership. This is not to be interpreted as "lording it over others." Such power politics is outside the scope of the Gospel. Persons are ordained for service. All ordained ministers share in the priesthood of all Christians by virtue of their baptism. They also share the priesthood of Christ in another dimension by virtue of their call and the sacrament they have received at ordination. Through this latter sacrament they are indelibly sealed with the priesthood of Jesus Christ for ministry.[2]

There is a difference in kind between the priesthood flowing from baptism and that flowing from ordination. It is not just a question of degrees.[3] But the charism of ordination is for others, not for oneself. All charisms are given for building the Church, and so it is with ordination.

The Universal Priesthood of the Laity

The relationship between ordained priesthood and the Eucharist is well known. The relationship of lay priesthood and the Eucharist is yet to be fully explored. The Orthodox perspective is very clear in this area. Everyone offers the sacrifice of the Eucharist. But it is one and the same offering as the one Christ offered on Calvary in time, and the one he continues to offer eternally in heaven.

The sacrifice of Jesus becomes ours through the Eucharist. It is not so much a matter of offering something new, or something old over and over. It is a matter of God's gift to us and our reception of the gift. There is an exchange of gifts. God's gift is received, and our gift is given. Not as though God were wanting. Rather we are in need until we have given praise and thanks to God for all his blessings through Jesus Christ.

Sacrament of Self-giving

At the heart of the Eucharist is the self-giving of Jesus Christ. That self-giving expresses the love of the Son of God for the Father and his willingness "in obedience" to undergo death "for us and our salvation."

The Letter to the Hebrews makes very clear that at the heart of the mystery of salvation is the self-giving of Jesus Christ (10:5-10). "Greater love than this no one has, that he lay down his life for his friends" (John 15:13). And Jesus laid down his life for us when we were sinners.

Jesus teaches us to give our selves to God as he did. He teaches us to accept the Father's will in obedience. If we live the Gospel, we will inevitably bear our cross with Christ. Accepting this cross "daily" is living the mystery of Christ in our own lives.

At the heart of the life and death of Jesus Christ is the mystery of his cross. Philippians indicates that it was *because* he emptied himself even to accepting the cross that Jesus was exalted by the Father with a name beyond all others: Lord (Phil 2:9-11). The Christian must share the same *kenosis* to inherit the resurrection with Christ and in Christ.

The Eucharist makes real, present, and active this essential paradigm of our faith. It is a renewal of the covenant between God and his people, the sharing in the cross of Christ and its ritual offering, putting on the mind of Christ, the transformative power of the Spirit.

At the heart of this mystery of the Eucharist is the exercise of priesthood, the priesthood of Christ. Priesthood and sacrifice are correlative. There must be a priest to offer sacrifice. And we share in both the priesthood and the sacrifice of Jesus. The holy and living sacrifice we offer is our self-offering together with the self-offering of Jesus.

An Antidote to Selfishness

Our age and culture needs to rediscover a selfless spirit. It is present in every human life but has been lost in large measure as a cultural value. Rugged individualism has led to rugged selfishness. "What's in it for me?" has replaced the view that "it is blessed to give rather than receive" (Acts 20:35).

We rediscover who we are by recovering worship and adoration. God is self-giving love. We become more fully ourselves, children of God, by imitating God's self-giving.

The child is dependent upon the self-giving of the parents. Siblings need each other. Society cannot survive on selfishness. Great literature recalls heroic deeds, acts of self-giving in which heroes have risen to critical occasions and gave themselves in heroic measure. Thermopolae, Sparta, Gettysburg were the scenes of heroism. Men confronted with utter destruction gave their all in a desperate effort marked by full faith in a cause.

Jesus Christ on Calvary was a hero. He accepted his own death "for the forgiveness of sins" and the salvation of all human kind. Death by human measure is defeat. But Jesus defeated death by accepting it. Because he humbled himself accepting ignominious death on a cross, *therefore* God exalted him, giving him the name of Lord (Phil 2:5-11). He thus became the firstfruits of salvation and the sign of hope for us all.

Sacrifice of the Church

The Eucharist is the sacrifice of the Church, head and members. The sacrifice of Christ on Calvary was complete. It obtained our salvation. Now we offer with Christ "a holy and living sacrifice" so that salvation may be ours. The sacrifice of Jesus is complete, but it is not ours until we have accepted it. Luther said the Eucharist is far more God's gift than our offering. We are in a receptive mood more than an active one.[4]

We are in the midst of mystery. This does not mean we cannot understand. It simply means we cannot exhaust all that this mystery holds. As in all things human, we come to the point of contemplation when words are inadequate. We speak theology, but we do not exhaust the mystery.

The ultimate criterion for truth is not our need or feelings, but God's glory. The priesthood of the laity and ordained ministry are interrelated for the glory of God. Both are needed so that God may be fully praised and thanked. Thus his glory is achieved.

In all liturgical prayer Christ is the high priest. He is the mediator. He is the great priest who offers sacrifice not that we may be saved from sickness, accident, failure; but that we may be saved from sin, self-destruction and idolatry.

The greatest danger is not our failure. The greatest danger is our sin; that we make ourselves into graven images of the devil who would not serve. God has made us icons of himself and his Son, that we might serve him with praise and love.

Thomas Aquinas continues to speak to us today. He expressed in his masterful treatise on the virtue of religion (Summa Theol. II-II q.81-100) how and why we must worship. Not for God's need, but to be true to ourselves.

The Eucharist Makes the Church

The Eucharist is the sacrifice of the Church. It is Christ the head, we the members: ordained and non-ordained. We offer together a sacrifice of praise and thanksgiving, of reparation and petition.

This sacrifice is pleasing to the Father because it is the self-offering of Jesus. With that self-offering we unite our own. We pray for the hallowing of God's name (i.e., that he will be praised for all he accomplishes in our world and in our history). We pray for the coming of his kingdom. It has already come, especially after the coming of Jesus Christ, the light and savior of the world. But we pray for its realization in our time, and its ultimate realization when the Lord comes in glory. The Eucharist looks forward to that eschatological time. The Eucharist anticipates the parousia and celebrates in sacrament: until he comes.

We offer the sacrifice in a prayer that God's will be sought and done. The infinite and wise plan of the Creator is only gradually revealed and in limited measure. But knowing that overarching plan and our part in it, is important to our success as human beings and to our salvation.

Our petitions for bread, forgiveness, strength in temptation, deliverance from evil are the daily stuff of any prayer. They are our basic needs. We ask for them after we have prayed for God's glory.

The Eucharist is the sacrifice of the Church in the ancient sense that the Church makes the Eucharist and the Eucharist makes the Church. This thought is richly developed in the liturgy and tradition of the East. In that perspective God's kingdom has come and will come. But we are distracted from its perception by many things, most of all by our spiritual blindness. Faith gives us the light to see the world as it is: God's world, of which we are a part. The world is not for us, it is for God, as we are. "All things are yours; and you are Christ's and Christ is God's" (1 Cor 3:22).

As the Church is gathered in assembly ("gathered as Church") to make the Eucharist, this very gathering and the sacramental action make the Church come alive. The complaint that our revised and renewed liturgies have not "caught on" are valid. Perhaps this is so because we have not realized the full importance of what we do and what we celebrate. Calvary and Easter become ours, part of our life as we gather to celebrate with our Lord.

Perhaps we celebrate too often, or too casually, or too routinely. Our Sunday Eucharist should especially be something well prepared, nurtured, and done with great care. The purpose of singing is to enhance the liturgical action with an atmosphere of symbol and aesthetic beauty. Our religion in the West is far too cerebral. We need to let the heart speak and sing, the imagination play its part, the intelligence guide us as we try to worship God with "a holy and living sacrifice."[5]

It must be a sacrifice vibrating with the holiness of Jesus, the angels and saints. It must be a living sacrifice: an offering of what we are living. A sacrifice of the lived Gospel. The sacrifice is ours. But it is holy because it is Christ's. It is living because it gives us life. It gives life to us as individual Christians and as the living body of Jesus Christ.

That body was born on the cross, from the side of Christ from which flowed blood and water (as humanity came from the side of Adam and the womb of Eve). That body lives in Christians of all ages. It lives in the young and the old. It lives in those who are ill and those who are well. It lives in the saint and the sinner (and we are both). It lives in us and in those before us, and those who are yet to come. At the Lord's table patriarchs and prophets, seers and sages, virgins and wives, orphans and widows of all time gather with us to say "Holy, holy, holy is the God of heavenly hosts. Heaven and earth are filled with God's glory."

Sacraments for People

In sacramento is the term used by Augustine and Aquinas. This is not jargon, this is an appeal to the world of symbol. The icon is not merely a representation. Its purpose is to bring the viewer to the experience of the composer. So it is with the music of Mozart or Beethoven. Each conductor interprets, each orchestra makes live, each musician thrills and conveys to the audience the ecstatic joy of the composer as he discovers the marvel and mystery of sound. There is more than understanding here (indeed there may be no understanding at all) but there is appreciation of the sheer beauty of sound, harmony, counterpoint, and rhythm.

To celebrate in sacraments is to celebrate in sacred signs. When our liturgy becomes prosaic and ponderous it fails as a vehicle for conveying the divine. The error since Trent is to believe that *ex opere operato* the sacraments will have their effect. They will . . . but how minimally! Often we come to Church to hear a symphony and are treated to a solo on the bassoon. We come for a full spectrum of sights and sounds and are given a perfunctory set of gestures and words that minimally do what is needed but little more.

This is the gathering of salvation. This is the gathering of the Church (*ekklesia*—those who are called/assembled by God for a share in salvation). Could we keep young people away if they really understood what is going on?

A Love Feast in the Spirit

In the Eucharist we all exercise our baptismal priesthood through Jesus Christ and his body which is the Church. Ordained ministers preside at the banquet, orchestrate the sounds, sights, gestures, and overall effect. But we must feast at the table. However poor the sign, the reality is the paschal mystery of the Lord that is brought to our altars so that we may feast with Christ in the love of the Holy Spirit.

Any love affair can be prosaic or pedantic if the lovers will allow it to be so. It will be as exciting and thrilling as they make it to be. And so it is with a banquet. Food is food. But the care and garnishing of the meal make it a feast for the eyes as well as for the taste. Food must be met with people who want to eat, who come with appetite and expectation . . . and joy. In the final analysis the Christian who comes to the Eucharist must come with a life and a spirit. The life he/she lives is what is offered. The spirit one cultivates is the hunger and thirst for God which is fed at his table.

Priesthood was a very controversial topic at the time of the Reformation. Luther believed a reevaluation of the common priesthood of the baptized was essential for the kind of renewal the Church needed. He believed the Church had become altogether too clericalized. This was especially true with regards to the Eucharist. Instead of the banquet of celebration, the Eucharist had become the priest's sacrifice, recited in Latin, in silence and even at times without the presence of anyone else.

Unfortunately in the heat of polemics some exaggerated the claim about the priesthood of the laity to the point of denying the sacramentality of ordination. Ordination, in the Protestant scheme of things, is the call of the Church and the congregation to serve as a leader, a preacher, and a teacher of the word.

Priesthood, Clericalism, and Authority

The emerging convergence on the Eucharist is a part of a larger convergence on baptism, Eucharist, and ministry. The latter should engage our attention at this point.

In the ARCIC *Final Report* ordination and authority, as well as Eucharist are discussed. There is an intimate relationship between all of these issues.

The Catholic position is that Jesus established his Church on the apostles. It was from the beginning hierarchically constituted. While the free churches and others have difficulty in accepting a clerical structure, it was part of the Church's self-understanding for over a thousand years.

Hierarchical structure and clericalism are two very different things. Clericalism means the cleavage between laity and clergy to the point of exaggeration. As with all "isms," there is an excess at work. Keeping an appropriate balance between the roles assigned to clerics in the Church and those assigned to the laity is of great importance.

The Reformers believed the Church had become far too clericalized. The abuses and excesses of clerical raw power and the denigration of the laity to the status of second-class citizens called for reform. Clerics in the late Middle Ages, especially in the papal states, were assigned to positions that properly belonged to the laity. The clergy tended to dominate society and to be involved in political and secular pursuits. Hence the tension in the Church about the proper function and use of authority. It was clear to all at the time of the Reformation (as it is today) that authority was required in the Church. The *manner* of its exercise was questioned.

Today, better than ever, we understand that there is no "divine right of kings" and the power of authority in the Church needs to be seen in terms of service. The Gospels are clear: "It must not be so among you" (Mark 10:43). Authority is not to become power over the lives of others. It is always to be the service of others and the service of the Gospel.

Part of the ecumenical agenda is the sorting out of the question of authority.[6] It is a vital need. In our culture and world authority is shared. The authority of the governing is subject to election and recall by the governed. Checks and balances assure that authority will not be excessive and must be responsible.

The Catholic position is that those who exercise priesthood over the body of Christ which is the Eucharist also exercise authority over the mystical body of Christ, which is the Church. Though there may be some question about the structure of the Church at the time of the apostles, it is clear that by the end of the first and surely the second century no one presided at the Eucharist unless they were recognized as having authority in the Church.

If we can rediscover the important nexus between authority and service, in the paradigm of John's Gospel which emphasizes the basin of water and the towel rather than the bread and cup, we may come a long way on the ecumenical road to the celebration of the sacrifice and priesthood instituted by Jesus Christ.

The Priesthood of the Laity

It will be difficult for the Church, Catholic and Protestant, to divest itself of its investment in clericalism. This will be easier for the Protestant Churches because the Reformation already was an attack on sixteenth-century clericalism. The Geneva Reformers especially were keen on introducing a church structure that would be more lay oriented and egalitarian.

The Eucharist is *not* the priest's thing, i.e., it is not first and foremost something clerical. This statement flies in the face of Tridentine doctrine and practice. However Vatican II, particularly in its revision of the liturgy makes it abundantly clear that the liturgy belongs to the people. This is the guiding principle of the reform, i.e., that the people might participate, not as passive spectators, but as active participants in the liturgy (SC # 10).

If the liturgical reform of Vatican II has failed thus far, it is largely because of the ingrained and difficult to eradicate perception that the liturgy belongs to the clergy. We have made much progress in this regard, but far from enough.

Participation, as Paul Bernier points out,[7] is too often seen as something optional. It seems *ad bene esse,* something that would make the Liturgy "better" but not essential to the liturgy. This view would never have prevailed for the first thousand years of Christianity. Participation of all those attending the Liturgy was normal.

With the emergence of vernacular languages participation became less and less possible. With the clericalization of the liturgy, participation was even considered undesirable by many.

The theology of the Liturgy from the twelfth century onward was of a liturgical "drama" rather than a sacramental communion sacrifice. Sacrifice was understood as "reenactment" much as a historical play would "reenact" a historical event. This view and theology is still not dead, though it has received a mortal wound from Vatican II. The implementation of the "new liturgy" continues, but not without difficulty. Indeed there are some who see the revised liturgy as the source of the present problems in the Church.[8]

Participation as Essential

In the view of Vatican II (and indeed of the long Christian tradition) Liturgy is the work of the Church. It is essentially the "work" of Jesus Christ (the great *leitourgos*), head of the body, which is the Church. Liturgy is also the "work" of the whole Christ, of the members of the mystical body.[9] Participation is therefore not an option but essential to the liturgy. If we are members of the body of Christ, we must be involved in what head and members are doing in worship.

In this respect the rediscovery of the priesthood of the laity is fortuitous. This theological reality gives the foundation for participation in the liturgy. By baptism we are incorporated into the body of Christ. And so when the mystical body worships through the liturgy, the whole body is involved. Active participation simply makes this priesthood active and visible as the liturgy evolves. Hence the importance of shared roles in the liturgy: lectors, ministers of song, hospitality, and Communion.

Ordained Priesthood and Laity

Vatican II tried to clarify the relationship between ordained and non-ordained ministry. It did not complete the task. However, it did give the foundation for this relationship, namely service.

The very nature of ordained ministry is service. As Christ was the servant of all, he commanded that those who have authority in the Church understand that authority is identical with service. Authority is given for service.

The task of ordained ministry, in terms of liturgy, is to aid, facilitate, and make possible the active participation of the laity. This perception of the role of the ordained is still not universally appreciated. In the measure that it is not, liturgy fails to be celebrated in the way it should according to Vatican II directives.

In a clerical view of liturgy the introduction of the laity is an intrusion. In the Vatican II view of liturgy the introduction of the laity into the liturgy is a necessity. You simply cannot have liturgy without it. "Solo work on the bassoon" is not the paradigm of the new liturgy.

Priesthood and Sacrifice

The correlation of priesthood and sacrifice can be helpful to viewing lay participation in the Eucharist. If the laity truly share in the priesthood of Christ, then they are called to offer sacrifice with him and in him. This is the only valid theological view of liturgy, given the principles and insights of Vatican II.

The task of clergy as celebrants and homilists is to help the laity to understand their essential role in the Eucharist. The laity have something to offer . . . indeed very much. They offer with Jesus the sacrifice of the entire Mystical Body. They "remember," i.e., present "before God" (with all the overtones that this expression has in Old Testament literature) the eternal sacrifice of Jesus, the Risen Lord. They receive that sacrifice as their own and "add to it" (by way of reception) their own lives as sacrificial offering.

This is not a duplication of the liturgical action of the clergy. It is an appropriation and participation in that action. Indeed the ordained priesthood exists *precisely* (in the Vatican II view of things) to facilitate this action/appropriation/participation of the laity.

1. The prophecy of Malachi is important to the patristic development of sacrifice. The sacrifice of Jesus appears in their writings as the fulfillment of Malachi's prophesy about the "perfect" sacrifice being offered in messianic times.

2. Some Protestant denominations do not accept the view that Ordination is a sacrament. They reserve the term sacrament for the Eucharist and Baptism, clearly in the New Testament. They call other sacred rites of the Church's Tradition "ordinances," i.e., rites for the good order of the Church. Marriage and sometimes the Anointing of the Sick are viewed in this light. The World Council of Churches' Faith and Order document *Baptism, Eucharist and Ministry* tries to bring a convergence between these views of ordained ministry. The subject is also taken up in bilateral conversations that have reached a greater consensus, as e.g., ARCIC I. *The Final Report* and the Lutheran World Federation-Roman Catholic document *Facing Unity*.

3. Vatican II, *Lumen Gentium*, #10.

4. Martin Luther, WA 6,369; LW 35,99 quoted by R. Crocken, *Luther's First Front*, 20–21.

5. Words from the Eucharistic Prayer of the Revised (Paul VI) Roman Missal, no. 3.

6. ARCIC I. *The Final Report* studies this issue in great depth. The Lutheran-Roman Catholic *Facing Unity* also touches the subject. The WCC Faith and Order *Baptism, Eucharist and Ministry* reaches a convergence in its treatment of ordained ministry.

7. Paul Bernier, *Ministry in the Church: A Historical and Pastoral Approach* (Mystic, Conn.: Twenty-Third Publications, 1992) 279–93.

8. One readily thinks of the Lefebvre movement which rejected Vatican II and moved into schism by the ordination of separatist bishops.

9. Pius XII, *Mediator Dei* (Encyclical on the Liturgy, 1947) made this point abundantly clear.

6   The Eucharist, the Spirit, and the Kingdom (Eschatology)

This chapter develops three important aspects of eucharistic theology: the Eucharist as sign of the kingdom *(eschatology)*, the eucharist as transformation by the Holy Spirit *(epiclesis)*, and the Holy Spirit, the sanctifier and gift of Father and Son to us in the Eucharist.

The Sign of the Kingdom

I have emphasized in several quotations from Orthodox writers, especially Alexander Schmemann, how the reality of the kingdom of God should influence our thinking and acting. In the measure that we understand and realize that we are in God's world, a part of his creation, in that measure will we appreciate our personal and collective salvation history.

In a platonic and neo-platonic world such a view of things was easier. In that philosophy the world we can see and experience is only the shadow of the reality we cannot see but experience through faith. God's kingdom comes. We pray for it in the Lord's Prayer so that we may be a part of it, may enhance its beauty and reality.

The Holy Spirit figures importantly in this world-view. He is the Creator Spirit. He hovered over the waters and the universe was born. He brought about the new age and the new creation by hovering over the Virgin Mary who gave birth to the Son of God through the Spirit's creative work.[1]

The Holy Spirit hovered over the Twelve as they gathered in the Upper Room waiting for the promise of the Risen Lord. The Holy Spirit came and filled the infant Church with his power and creative gifts. This small band of followers went out into the world to announce the good news of the coming of the kingdom of grace through the sending of God's Spirit in fidelity to the promise of Jesus Christ, the Risen Lord and Son of God.

"It is important for you that I go. Because if I do not go, the Holy Spirit will not come. . . ." (John 16:7). With the ascension of Jesus as Lord sitting at the right hand of the Father, begins the age of the Holy Spirit. His mission is to sanctify the Church. The Spirit helps us to understand the words of Jesus and that we are, by grace, adopted children of the Father, able to say "Abba" and "Jesus is Lord" (Rom 8:15 and 1 Cor 12:3).

The Orthodox Witness

Contact with the Orthodox understanding of the Eucharist makes one more aware of the importance of the theme of the kingdom in Christian theology. That theme is clearly a dominant theme of the New Testament. Luke announces Jesus as coming to the synagogue at Nazareth, and reading the text of Isaiah about the coming of messianic times. "This day, this scripture is fulfilled in your hearing," he tells them (4:21). "The kingdom is at hand. Repent and believe the good news" (Mark 1:15) is Mark's description of the New Testament theme.

Inexorably God's kingdom comes. When we pray for its coming in the Lord's Prayer, we ask that we may be a part of it, that it may come in us, for us, and by us. The coming of the kingdom is synonymous with the coming of the reign of God, eternal life for all who are saved.

For the Orthodox this kingdom is brought about specifically and particularly by the Eucharist. The Church is where salvation takes place. It is more than the institutional Church, or the Church here and now. It is identical with the communion of saints. It extends to all times and places, *ab Abel justo* (from the time of the just Abel) until the Lord comes again in glory.

The kingdom is Augustine's "City of God," the body of Christ, the temple being built of living stones by a living and holy sacrifice. It is the living God giving life through grace. The living and Risen Lord gives divine life through the gift of his sanctifying Spirit.

For the Orthodox entering liturgy is entering this world of the divine. It is more than a utopian "dream world" to which one takes refuge, away from the cares and worries of this world.

The Gospel is clear: the reign of God is within you (in your midst) (Luke 17:21). It is the world of the Spirit, but also the real world in which we live and move and have being. The purpose of liturgy is to make us more conscious of it, more dynamically in contact with God's kingdom. Thus the Lord's Prayer is realized even as we pray.

The Holy Spirit and the Eucharist

We begin to understand the role of the Holy Spirit in the Eucharist as we understand the Spirit's role in the Church. The Spirit prepares the final, glorious coming of God's kingdom. That kingdom is not identified with the institutional Church. It is rather identified with all those who come to believe in God and come to salvation.

Post-conciliar documents of the Church underscore that the Holy Spirit is at work not only in the Catholic Church or in Christianity. The Spirit "blows where it wills" (John 3:8). And there is evidence that the Spirit "blows" even in other religious traditions beyond the Jewish and Christian.

The Spirit is the Sanctifier. Jesus, the Son of God is the Savior. He redeemed the world on the cross, "for the forgiveness of sins." He rose from the grave and thus his humanity achieved its full glory. He ascended to the Father. Now he continues to send his Spirit to those who are open to his coming.

The Spirit is given to all the baptized. Thus they are incorporated into the body of the Risen Lord. Of that body, the soul is the Holy Spirit. That body grows into likeness and fullness of the mature Christ. We grow as members of the body of Christ through the creative and sanctifying action of the Holy Spirit.

The Spirit and the Liturgy

The West generally has not given sufficient attention to the Holy Spirit in the celebration of the Eucharist and in its Eucharistic theology. "The Great Unknown" is much more in the consciousness of Eastern Christians.

The New Testament makes it clear that as Jesus, the Risen Lord, ascends into heaven, he sends a new Paraclete, a new person with a new mission, that of sanctifying the Church and the world. The mission of Jesus is ended. He takes his place in glory. This is not to say that he is no longer with us or interested in human history. Jesus is the head of the Church. He is with us always, especially where two or three are gathered in his name for prayer. But his saving action is done through the gift of the Holy Spirit, the abiding guest and sanctifier.

The Acts of the Apostles makes it clear that, after the ascension of the Lord, we are in the age of the Spirit. This book has been called the Gospel of the Holy Spirit. The Book of Revelation also speaks of the work of the Spirit in the Churches.

Epiclesis

Throughout the liturgical history of the Church, the work of the Spirit in the Eucharist has been emphasized in the anaphora or Eucharistic prayer. These prayers, especially in the East, stress that it is the creative Spirit who transforms the bread and wine into the body and blood of Jesus Christ. This same Spirit transforms those who receive the body and blood of Christ through grace. Thus they become more fully and really the mystical body of Christ.

The transforming action of the Spirit is what the Church is all about. It is not a bureaucracy or mere hierarchy. It is the living body of the Risen Lord. This body, the kingdom, continues to be created by the work of the sanctifying Spirit.

The Spirit is particularly at work as we "remember" what the Lord did on the night he died. The Spirit helps us to understand *what he did* and what he wants us to do. It is the example of Jesus we must repeat, much more than his words. And the sanctifying Spirit is required for us to build the kingdom, for without this Spirit we can do nothing.

The Spirit is the source of all that is good, all that is true, all that is beautiful. Through the Eucharist the Spirit transforms bread and wine, but more importantly he transforms Christians, making them instruments of Christ for the building of the kingdom.

Epiclesis in Ecumenical Convergence

The BEM document recovers for the West the importance of the epicletic dimension of the Eucharist. The Eucharist is the work of the

Holy Spirit, transforming bread and wine into the body and blood of Christ. This transforming activity is not simply in order to have the presence of Christ on the altar as an object of adoration. The bread and wine are transformed so that Christians may be transformed from children of Adam to children of God, reborn by the grace of the New Adam through the transforming power of the Holy Spirit.

The epicletic action of the Holy Spirit, for the East, is the very essence of the transformation of the elements. Rather than an emphasis on the words of institution as a "consecrating formula" the East has seen the entire liturgy as transformation.

Vatican II stresses that the Eucharist does not make present Jesus Christ who was absent before the consecration. He is present in his Church "assembled as Church/*ekklesia*." He is present in the minister. He is present and speaking as the Scriptures are read. He is present in the faithful as they gather and pray in his name.

When the transformation of the elements takes place Jesus is present in a new and eminent way *(sacramentaliter)*. As Thomas Aquinas explained so well, not as in a place but in the way a substance is present in something, e.g., bread. Wherever bread is present, the same "substance" is present. It can be wheat, corn, barley; thick or thin, sweet or sour, leavened or unleavened. It is all bread and it is present as such.

Catholic tradition explains that we do not have words to express the mystery and the sublime truth of what it means to have God among us, Christ with us "until the end of time" in this unique and central sacrament we call the Eucharist.[2] But that presence is not simply for contemplation. It is for action, i.e., the action of the transforming Spirit. The epicletic action extends through the sacrament to human beings. The Spirit sanctifies.

We are sanctified in many ways. Most importantly by our living of the Gospel. The virtuous acts of the just are the "works" of the Holy Spirit. The Gospel takes flesh as we forgive sinners, give comfort to the sick, extend our selves, our time, our talents and energy in the service of others. Whatever we do for those in need, we do for Christ. And thus we build the Kingdom of God.

The inspiration and power to do all these things comes from the Holy Spirit. As he hovered over the universe in creation, so he hovers over the world in its sanctification and transformation. This does not mean that the kingdom has come. It is coming, however. It will come in full glory at the end of time when the Lord Jesus comes to take it up in a final offering to the Father.

In this view the Holy Spirit is not someone we nod to on the feast of Pentecost. He is a divine person continually at work in our world and in our hearts. The Spirit is the gift of the Father. He was promised to the Son. The Son in heaven now claims that promise and in turn sends (with the Father) their Spirit to his Church and to the world.

The Creative Spirit

Yves Congar has a long theological reflection on the epicletic dimension of the Eucharist in his tract *I Believe in the Holy Spirit*.[3] The ecumenical convergence document, *Baptism, Eucharist and Ministry* underscores the importance of this dimension of the Eucharist.[4]

Given the extraordinary influence of the charismatic movement on the Church today, and the theological significance of important reflections on the Holy Spirit and the Spirit's role in the spiritual life, we need to reflect at some length on this dimension of the Eucharist and its relationship to spiritual growth.

Eschatology

The kingdom to come is also called the *eschata* (the last things). The Gospels, and also the writings of Paul, Peter, and the Book of Revelation speak of the end of the world. The last things to happen before the Lord comes again in glory.

We have emphasized the power of this truth on the Early Church. For the immediate followers of Christ, the second coming was imminent. Paul talks about who will be left to greet the Lord when he comes again in glory (1 Thess 4:13-18).

Various letters of the New Testament were written to clarify that only the Father knows the day and the hour. If the event seems to delay in coming, this does not mean that Christians should be less alert and *en garde*.

The Advent liturgy is filled with an acute awareness that Christians must ever prepare "the coming of the Lord." This alert awaiting is characteristic of the Christian. With faith to see the world as God's kingdom, and the parousia as always imminent (with God a thousand years are as a day, and a day as a thousand years (2 Pet 3:8).

This eschatological perspective determines very much how one lives. If there is "no tomorrow," then we should "eat, drink and be merry, for tomorrow we die" (Isa 22:13). But if the parousia is as certain as the day and the dawn, then we should live in expectation that the Lord will come to judge the world.

The Second Coming of Christ

Just as the ecumenical convergence on the Eucharist has rediscovered its epicletic dimension, so has it found anew the importance of eschatology. Eschatology is the study of the "last things" (heaven, hell, judgment, etc.) The New Testament writings are full of this concept of the Lord's return in glory. For these writers the event was imminent. Even though Paul reproves those who are unwilling to work because they want to prepare for the Lord's imminent coming, he tells them that those who are unwilling to work should not eat (2 Thess 3:10).

Whatever the exact nature of the expectation of the New Testament writers, they were obviously mistaken about the imminent nature of that coming. As time wore on, Christianity paid less and less attention to this dimension of the Christian message. Advent does provide a time for reflecting upon the second coming of Christ, but that reflection quickly gives way to the joyful celebration of Christmas.

Theologically, however, eschatology was in need of rediscovery. Though we still are no more "in the know" about the exact time of the "rapture/coming" there is a value in seeing the *eschaton* as an important perspective for life—any time. Keeping our ultimate goal in sight helps us to "be alert," to "be sober and watch" lest the day of the Lord's coming catch us by surprise (1 Pet 5:8).

Modern theologians have raised our consciousness of the vital importance of an eschatological perspective. Our idea of the end will color our determination of the means to get there. Our understanding of the link between the first and second coming of Christ will help us to understand the "in between time" that we are living each day.

Eucharist and Eschatology

Geoffrey Wainwright in his classic *Eucharist and Eschatology*[5] has made a case for the importance of this dimension of the Eucharist. The Apostolic Church was more aware of this dimension as they gathered around the altar to "remember the death of the Lord until he comes" (1 Cor 11:26). We should grasp this dimension of the Eucharist as we follow their example.

The purpose of creation itself and our existence must be described theologically as achieving the glory of God. As with all creation, our very existence testifies to God's creating and regenerating power.

The Holy Spirit enables us through grace and faith to perceive God in creation and in our hearts. The Spirit teaches us that "Jesus is Lord" and that God is our Father. The Spirit prays in us in divine whispers. Thus we can enter into that praise and thanks of God which finds its highest expression in the thanksgiving of the glorified Jesus before the throne of the Father. The Book of Revelation recalls this hymn of glory as does the Letter to the Hebrews and other works of Scripture.

When we celebrate the Eucharist, we essentially are moved by the Holy Spirit and join, in Christ, the eternal praise of all creation and all the angels and saints in their hymn of praise and thanksgiving to God for his marvelous works.

The Eucharist is the symbol of the heavenly banquet. In Orthodox terminology the Eucharist is God's gift to us of the "antepast," the foretaste of the heavenly banquet itself. "Taste and see that the Lord is good" (Ps 34:8). While we are more aware that the parousia is not yet, we are encouraged by the Scriptures to "watch and wait" for we know not the day or the hour (Matt 25:13).

The perception of Teilhard de Chardin of a world moving inexorably toward *point omega,* when the Lord shall come in glory needs to be recalled in this context. Rather than seeing technological progress and human progress as inimical to spiritual progress, Teilhard was able to see such progress as part of the Creator's ongoing development of the world and human development as related to the final triumph of the kingdom.[6]

"Eye has not seen, nor ear heard . . . what God has prepared for those who wait on him" (1 Cor 2:9). We see now "darkly as in a mirror" but then face to face (1 Cor 13:12). We are God's children but the full revelation of what that means must await heaven (1 John 3:2). And yet the Eucharist is the beginning of our experience of the "mystery" of Christ, that he is the promise of God and its fulfillment.

The mystics speak of "tasting God." And so the metaphor is that seeing and imagining may not be as productive in our efforts to understand and experience the Eucharist as touching, feeling, and hearing. We hear God's Word, and it reassures us of the things to come. In the Eucharist we touch and taste the transformed bread and cup and know that we have shared communion with God.

The Eucharist is more in the line of a symphony than a lecture. A conductor confessed he did not understand Prokofiev. Yet he enjoyed conducting him. Music is the vicarious experience of the thrill of the composer; now it is shared by the conductor, the orchestra and the audience. Sight, sound, rhythm, and counterpoint are all blended in a marvelous experience of the composer's joy.

And so it is with the Eucharist. The Lord left us a testament (Luther's favorite word). He left us a promissory note that he would deliver when we "remember him . . . until he comes." And so we pray that when the symbol is recalled we may receive a share in the promise.

The Holy Spirit is the love of God, the holiness of God within us, the Indwelling Guest. In us the Spirit makes known Christ and ourselves, Christ as the Son of God, we as God's beloved children. We know who we are because we know whence we came and our destiny. Our Divine Guest is the source of all inspiration. He is the "creative spirit" bringing about all good inspirations and all creative energy.

Yves Congar is pleased to note, with *Gaudium et Spes* that theologians and creative artists and others who influence culture need to be in touch with each other. They are inspired by the same Spirit who works all good things and truth in our world.[7]

The Spirit is not restricted to our Church or our faith. The Spirit works in other Churches and other faiths. Indeed he works in those who have no faith at all, yet seek to promote what is good and true and beautiful.

A Monastic View

This writing has been made possible thanks to a generous invitation to join the monks of St. Benedict at St. John's University and the

Institute for Ecumenical and Cultural Research. During my months at Collegeville, I have come to better appreciate living in a rural environment with the rhythms of the liturgy and a realization of living in the world that God made. Away from the urban world and concern about economics and sociology and politics (though one does not escape these realities even in a monastery) one better appreciates this world of the Church and of faith.

Nature and liturgy combine to refine and reappropriate the culture in which we live. One need not be absorbed in television, movies, media, and the trivia of daily living. One can find a deeper meaning to life. And that meaning is nurtured by faith.

In this surrounding I have come to a deeper appreciation of the daily Eucharist. The Eucharist can become the center and goal of life, "the source and summit of the Christian spirit," as Vatican II describes it (SC#10).

The Eucharist is the moment when the Risen Lord sends his Spirit to sanctify the gifts of bread and wine and those who use them. They become "apostles" and missionaries: sent to spread the good news and to build the kingdom.

---

1. Yves Congar, *I Believe in the Holy Spirit* (New York: Seabury, 1983) 2:218–20.

2. *Adoro Te Devote*

> Adoro te devote, latens Deitas,
> Quae sub his figuris vere latitas:
> Tibi se cor meum totum subjicit
> Quia te contemplans, totum deficit.

> Jesu quem velatum nunc aspicio
> Oro, fiat illud quod tam sitio:
> Ut te revelata cernens facie,
> Visu sim beatus tuae gloriae. Amen.

3. *Ibid.*

4. World Council of Churches, *Baptism, Eucharist and Ministry*, E# 14–18.

5. G. Wainwright, *Eucharist and Eschatology* (New York: Oxford).

6. Pierre Teilhard de Chardin, *The Phenomenon of Man* (New York: Harper and Row, 1959); *Hymn of the Universe* (New York: Harper and Row, 1965); *The Divine Milieu* (New York, Harper, 1968, 1960).

7. Y. Congar, *I Believe in the Holy Spirit*, 2:218–20.

7 The Eucharist and Spirituality

The salient idea of this book is that the Holy Spirit has guided Christians of all Churches to nourish their Christian life with the Eucharist. The idea of sacrifice has been understood in various ways. But like a rich mosaic made up of many various pieces these many insights can be gathered together for a deeper appreciation of this unique sacrament.

I would like to suggest in this chapter that the Eucharist can be a focal point for one's Christian spirituality. And if it is, some of the insights we have gleaned from our reflection on the Eucharist as sacrifice will be helpful in enriching that spirituality.

Spirituality is the tone of our Christian life. It is the poetry and the music. The "meat and potatoes" of our spirituality are the keeping of the commandments: "Do this and you shall live." "And what more can I do" and Jesus answered: "If you want to be perfect, go sell what you have and give it to the poor . . . and come, follow me" (Matt 19:21).

Eucharistic spirituality focuses on the love of Jesus Christ in instituting the Eucharist and abiding with us in the celebration and communion that flow from this sacrament. It is a rich spirituality because it stems from a contemplation of the sacrifice celebrated and the Communion received.

Many Christians down the ages and in many places today find in the Eucharist a focus for their spirituality. Mother Teresa of Calcutta and her community, the Little Brothers of Charles de Foucault, the Capuchin Franciscans among others find this orientation helpful. The Congregation of the Blessed Sacrament, founded by St. Peter Julian Eymard has this orientation, modeling its contemporary living on the example set in 1856 by St. Eymard at rue d'Enfer in Paris.

Sacrifice as Self-giving

The Eucharist as sacrifice reminds us of the gift of self of Jesus. He made it in the incarnation. It was consummated in the self-offering of Jesus to the Father's will on Calvary. This self-offering is the reason (as Philippians makes clear) why Jesus was made Lord and exalted to the right hand of the Father (2:5-11). Our task as Christians is to live our offering, and to offer our lives. Life and worship are but two sides of the coin, two phases of what we do as Christians. The idea that we can be Christians at home falls flat in this understanding.

We can worship at home. But the trumpeter cannot play the symphony unless he joins the orchestra. We cannot worship as the Body of Christ, "assembled as Church," unless we join the assembly. The reasons are more than aesthetic or social. They are profoundly theological, liturgical, and human.

Sacramenta propter homines (the sacraments are for men and women) is a time-honored saying. It means that sacraments should be celebrated in a human way, and pastors should be human in their administration of them. But there is another sense in which the saying is true. God understands in Jesus Christ, that we need sacraments. We need signs of God's approval. We need signs of God's grace and of his love.

We celebrate sacraments because we rejoice in God's love. We celebrate birth, death, marriage, adulthood, religious dedication, and forgiveness of sins. We need to see these not as a carrot to be held by the Church for compliance with its rules, but as gifts of God given generously and freely "so that we might live."

The sacraments are for men and women; not they for sacraments. Our pastoral approach to sacraments must start from the principle of human need and divine generosity. There must be nothing in our administration that begins to smack of power and the desire to "lord it over others." Our reception of the sacraments similarly must not stem from social need to do what others are doing, but from a desire to celebrate our relationship with God and our desire to deepen that relationship in love.

Eucharistic Contemplation (Adoration)

Eucharistic prayer outside the time of celebration is simply a recognition of the need to contemplate, to go more deeply, to open ourselves to God's revelation of himself, his love, and his ineffable greatness.

Eucharistic prayer, like Eucharistic sacrifice is not something God needs. It is something we need because we are God's creatures, his children. Husband and wife need expressions of love and affection to sustain and revitalize and express their intimate relationship to each other. Paul did well to liken the relationship of Christ to his Church, (and by implication the Eucharist and the Church) to that of husband and wife (Eph 5:32).

Eucharistic Spirituality after Vatican II

Our better understanding of the Eucharist as sacrifice should help us in our efforts to develop a spirituality centered in the Eucharist. When the Eucharist was considered more of a "spectator sport" and prayer before the exposed host, or the tabernacle was seen as a substitute for Communion, something was wrong. Even when, with the help of the Council of Trent, Eucharistic devotions were given more validity and doctrinal foundations, they were not entirely related to the Eucharist as sacrifice.

An integration of both is necessary and useful. We need to understand the centrality of the sacrificial dimension of the Eucharist. The sacrifice is the sacrifice of Jesus Christ. It is not so much the historical sacrifice of Calvary—though it is involved—but the "sacrifice" he presents eternally before the Father's throne and which pleads salvation for us.

This eternal prayer of praise and eternal sacrifice of propitiation we tap when we enter into Eucharistic contemplation. We continue the prayer of Jesus, we associate ourselves to it, we are moved by the Holy Spirit who prays in us to be a part of the never-ending prayer of Jesus.

As Rowan Williams explained so well in his Grove Liturgical Study,[1] the Eucharist makes us "worthy" to stand in God's presence where we serve God. This is true of the laity as well as the clergy, since we all share in the sacrifice and priesthood of Jesus Christ.

Rowan points out the challenge of this call to priesthood and its requirement of striving for holiness and justice.

Eymardian Spirituality

St. Peter Julian Eymard developed his own Christian life by focusing it on the Eucharist as the center, end, and means of the spiritual life. Pivotal to his spirituality was the idea of a gift of self. He shared that insight with many spiritual authors, especially those of the French School of Spirituality (Olier, Berulle, etc.)

On March 21, 1865, St. Eymard made a solemn vow and gift of himself to Jesus Christ in the Eucharist. He considered what he did on this Feast of St. Benedict of supreme importance for his spiritual life. The formulation for this gift of self was taken directly (and verbatim) from the writings of Jean Jacques Olier.[2] But the orientation and intent was particular. He wished to imitate the *kenosis,* the gift of self, which Jesus made in the incarnation. Thus he wanted Jesus to be the dominant force in his personality. He wanted Jesus "to live in me and I in him."

Learning from Our Ecumenical Friends

What have we learned from our ecumenical partners about the Eucharist as sacrifice, and how can we apply this learning to our spirituality? We have learned that sacrifice is essentially self-offering. Not that our offering is the most important. Rather the self-offering of Jesus is the essential element of the sacrifice. But we must accept his gift and respond to his grace and salvation. We must believe in his love and accept it.

The most important aspect of the Eucharist is not what happens to the bread, but what happens to us. We share the inner life of Jesus. That is important. This inner life of Jesus that flows through our souls also unites us to all those so united to Christ. We form a body of which the Spirit is the soul. And this body lives the paschal mystery every day, and in every time. What we offer at the altar is what we live in the streets.

Our liberation from sin is the reason why we work for the social liberation of all who are oppressed whether by personal sin or collective structures that cry to heaven for justice. As we contemplate the

Eucharist, we see and understand the mind of Christ who came to set us free and to bring peace to the world.

We learn from our ecumenical friends that the sacraments are signs of God's love and God's grace. We do not manipulate God. God saves us because God loves us. We do not accumulate points with God. All is gift. But if we have been so graced by a loving God, we need to respond to this love by love of others.

The Church is not for itself but for salvation. The concern of the Church should not be predominantly for its members but for those who are not. Christ did not come to save the saved or the self-righteous. He came to call genuine sinners. And that is the task of the Church: not to lay down laws, but to reach out in loving concern for those who are sinful, marginalized, oppressed, and guilty. In that context the Church and we must be more concerned about unity than about theological precision; more concerned about pastoral outreach and mission than about ecclesiastical turf. The Church, like Christ, must be more interested in salvation, than in government.

And from this must flow a spirituality which targets the poor, the oppressed, the sinful, the outcasts. We must be more concerned about those who are not in our Church than with those who are. In this way we will be in communion with Jesus who is in the Eucharist not for the just but for sinners. Only when we can identify the Church as sinful can we begin to understand why the Church is holy: because it is the place where salvation happens through Jesus Christ.

The Eucharist as Spirituality

From various understandings of the Eucharist through the ages have arisen a variety of Christian responses. The strong ecclesial and symbolic emphasis of the early Church led to a grounding of the spiritual life in the Eucharistic celebration and Communion.

In the Middle Ages an emphasis on the real presence of Jesus Christ under the appearances of bread and wine, led to the institution of the Feast of Corpus Christi and a spirituality growing out of Eucharistic contemplation and adoration. Processions, benediction of the Blessed Sacrament, the Forty Hours devotions, visits to the Blessed Sacrament were the outgrowth of this understanding and the expression in private devotions of the faith of the laity.

For some this phase of Eucharistic devotion is a corruption of authentic practice. They would advocate an abrogation of these devotions with a return to the original emphasis on the Eucharist as celebration and Communion.

The ecumenical convergence represented in BEM does not call for such an abrogation. It emphasizes that those who see the value of such devotions should not look down on those who do not. And similarly those who do not have such Eucharistic devotions should not begrudge those who have them.[3]

This chapter suggests there are excellent reasons for supporting such devotion and prayer. A spirituality centered on the Eucharist does not require such devotions, but it would certainly favor them.

The fundamental reason, as is well expressed in *Eucharisticum Mysterium* and *Eucharistiae Sacramentum,* is that they flow from the Liturgy and lead back to it.[4] Eucharistic celebration and Communion naturally invite the Christian to contemplate what was celebrated and what was received. This Eucharistic contemplation centers on the love of Christ "unto the end" and the love of the Father who "so loved the world . . ." and the Spirit who dwells in us and unites us in communion with Christ and with the Triune God.

Rather than suppress a spirituality which is centered on the Eucharist and nurtured by Eucharistic devotions, one should rather study and experience the value of such a spirituality for a full living of the Christian life. The fact that the Orthodox do not have such devotions (or spirituality) does not mean they cannot appreciate it. The same is true of main line Protestants as well.

Ecclesial Dimensions

A basic problem with contemporary Eucharistic spirituality generally is that it was built on an individualistic model. In the wake of Vatican II and thanks to its more ecclesial orientation, we are becoming more aware that we are saved first of all as a people, collectively. Only secondly and as a consequence are we saved individually. Our present individualistic culture (and the basic egoistical orientation of our sinful nature) make it hard to focus on the Church as the foundation of our spirituality.

The Eucharist remedies this problem in two ways. First it concentrates on the gathered people (the *ekklesia*) and helps us to see ourselves as members of the Church, the mystical body of Christ. Secondly (though of prior importance) the Eucharist uproots our basic egoism. The fruit *(res)* of the Eucharist is the unity of the Church, the body of Christ. The Eucharist builds the body of Christ by healing the wound of sin and by giving us "step by step" the glorification that will be ours fully in heaven.

The Eucharist, as J.-M.-R. Tillard states repeatedly,[5] has three purposes: communion with the Father in Christ and with our brothers and sisters, remission of sin, and a share in future glory. This share in the glory that awaits us is given us as an inheritance in baptism, but it grows with our growth in Christ.

Eucharist is therefore related to baptism as food is related to birth. The adult is in "germ" in the infant. But must be nurtured, must grow into the man or woman. The Christian is born into Christ through baptism but is nurtured into the full maturity of Christ through the Christian life, nurtured by the Bread of Life. Hence Jesus' words: "Unless you eat . . . you cannot have life. . . . Whoever eats . . . has everlasting life, and I will raise him up on the last day (John 6:53-58).

Eucharist and Ecclesiology

Again we are indebted to Jean Tillard for an insight into the intimate connection between the Eucharist and the Church. Following the teaching of Thomas Aquinas, Tillard observes that the Eucharist is not an individualistic approach to God in Christ. It is the Pasch of the Church. As such it is rooted, as all the sacraments are, in the life of the Church.[6]

This is precisely the important value of the Eucharist, its ultimate goal *res tantum* is the unity of the Church. It achieves this purpose by (negatively) removing our proclivity to sin and (positively) by giving us divine and eternal life. This immortality is given to us by the Risen Lord whose body became a "vivifying spirit" through his resurrection. Thus with Thomas Aquinas we see the cause of our death to sin in the death of Jesus, and our divinization and resurrection caused by the resurrection of Jesus.

As Tillard shows most effectively, this teaching is repeatedly presented by both the East and West, the Fathers of Alexandria and Antioch, the Greek and Latin Fathers. It is at the heart of the long tradition that is being recovered by the ecumenical convergence of our day.

In this context the Eucharist is at the very heart of the Church. The Eucharist "makes" the Church because it applies the salvation (soteriology) of Christ merited by his passion and death in its "first moment of salvation." The Eucharist makes the Church in its "second moment of salvation" by giving life divine and everlasting. In this second moment communion with the Father in Christ and the Spirit is at the heart of the matter. Through this union with the Trinity *en Christo* the members of the Church are united to one another (by the Spirit) as members of the body of Christ. Thus the Eucharist becomes the sign of unity. But this unity is not only among living Christians. It is also a unity among all those who ever lived (or who ever will live) in the communion of saints.[7]

In the Eucharistic liturgy heaven and earth are united in one universal hymn of praise and thanksgiving. (Hence the importance of the metaphor of symphony). Our culture has difficulty in appreciating the liturgy because it has difficulty in appreciating all the arts.[8] To many the arts are a waste of time. (We might say the same of sports, in view of its contribution to the common good).

However the arts are as important to the betterment of our world as the sciences. (We might say that sports—if they are not given exaggerated importance—also have a definite contribution to make). Music, poetry, the arts have a refining function that is too little appreciated (Congreve's line about music "soothing the savage beast"[9] comes to mind).

And so it is with liturgy. However there is more to liturgy than aesthetics. Liturgy is the worship of the people. It is as necessary to the human spirit as song is to birds and play to animals. St. Francis of Assisi could change the society in which he lived because he was able to see the divine in all of creation and could be its "troubadour," singing the praises of God in the name of all creatures.

In a world that is ego-centered and people-centered praise and adoration are a waste of time. But for monks who live close to nature and can appreciate the link between praising God and living in God's world, it is as necessary as breathing.

By focusing on the Eucharist, we can begin to understand the world from God's perspective. God loved the world and all of us from all eternity. That is why God sent Jesus, who loved us "to the end"

(John 13:1), even to dying on a cross for us. He left us the memorial of that love so that we might remember how much he loved us, and his commandment to love each other in like measure.

The Eucharist is the hymn of the universe (Teilhard de Chardin),[10] it is God's Son giving everlasting praise to the Father in our name and inviting us to join him and all creation in a magnificent symphony of God.

We have the choice to join in the chorus or to simply ignore the music. But we cannot do the latter with impunity. We have been called and given talents for the song of praise. We will be asked to give an account of what we have done with these talents.

A Holy and Living Sacrifice

The Eucharist is a holy and living sacrifice because it is the sacrifice of God's holy one, Jesus Christ. It is the self-offering of his life, death, and resurrection. It is a sacrifice most pleasing to the Father.

This sacrifice is given to us to offer with Christ and in him. Like the great classic composers, we have been given the score, the hymn to sing or play. Each of us must do so with our own talents, with the particular instrument we have a gift to play. Christ is the great conductor who has given us the directive: *con amore.*

This song must be sung in liturgy but lived in life. After the liturgy and flowing from it must be the life of the Christian. Our task is to take our song into the highways and byways. We are to turn song and inspiration into action.

The challenge of a world at war, in hate, surrounded by violence must be answered by Christian concern and sacrifice. Martyrdom may be the price we have to pay for our belief that life need not go on forever as it has thus far.

Christ came for every age. His salvation must be given anew in every age. Sin is ever present in every heart and in every person. Christ came to save us all.

The struggle of each is the struggle of "everyman." War, starvation, greed, lust, pride, hatred come to every time. The answer is in the Gospel and the grace of Jesus Christ. The Church is the place where salvation happens. This is not to canonize the institutional Church. For within that "city," as Augustine pointed out, the same struggle goes on as in the earthly city. There are those who surrender to the forces of evil even in lofty places in the Church.

But the body of Christ, the *qahal* Jaweh, is being built up by the Eucharist, by Christ who is with his people. He saves sinners, he comforts widows, he blesses children. Those who do not gather with Christ scatter (Matt 12:30).

He came to give glory to the Father and salvation to human-kind. He calls us to the same mission. As members of his body, we work for his kingdom. We spread the "good news." We work for unity among all who are similarly called.

The Eucharist is more than a sign of unity. It is the cause of unity. The Eucharist purifies each cell of the body of Christ, it nurtures the seed of immortality given at baptism. The Eucharist binds us to Christ and through the gift of his transforming Spirit, to the Father and to every living being.

Eucharistic Sharing

Whether the Church wishes to underscore the many things that continue to divide Christians by forbidding Eucharistic sharing, or whether it wants to emphasize the many more things that unite Christians in faith and Jesus Christ is for the Church to decide. For my part I believe it would be more productive for Christian unity to emphasize the latter. My reasons for believing this are profoundly theological as well as ascetical and ecumenical.

Theologically the reality of the Eucharist is such that whether we receive at the same altar or at separate altars we are inevitably being drawn into the body of Christ, the communion of saints. The Christ who binds us to himself in communion [see Paul Claudel][11] is stronger than our divisions or our canons. He brings us into unity de-spite our historical divisions and our reluctance to bring about the Church that our times require.

Ascetically I believe that the humility and "kenotic spirit"[12] that is required would do the Churches a great deal of good. It is one thing to say *mea culpa* in written documents. It is more believable and im-pressive to see actions that match one's words.

Ecumenically I believe the time has come to break down the ec-clesiastical "Berlin wall." We will never complete the work of unity until we begin to do it together. A breakthrough in this area would begin to say to the world that we believe that the work of unity is far more the work of Christ than of theologians and hierarchs. Perhaps when we have begun to receive the Eucharist at each other's altar, we will begin to see more clearly the other steps to which we are called to make the "real though imperfect communion" which is ours into *full communion.*

---

1. Rowan Williams, *Eucharistic Sacrifice: The Roots of a Metaphor,* Grove Liturgical Study #31 (Bramcote Notts, England: 1982).

2. Jean Jacques Olier, *Catéchisme Chrétien,* leçon XX (Migne, 1856) 478.

3. World Council of Churches, *Baptism, Eucharist and Ministry,* E#32.

4. *Eucharisticum Mysterium,* #50; *Eucharistiae Sacramentum,* #80 and #81. These two passages explain in detail how devotion to Christ in the Eucharist is related to the celebration of the Eucharist and the reception of Communion. They also show the connection with the Christian life and good deeds.

5. J.-M.-R. Tillard, *The Eucharist: Pasch of God's People* (Staten Island: Alba House, 1966).

6. Ibid.

7. Ibid.

8. Harvey Cox, *The Feast of Fools: A Theological Essay on Festivity and Fantasy* (Cambridge, Mass.: Harvard University Press, 1969). Cox develops some of these same insights. A recovery of memory and imagination are essential to the survival of our culture and religion.

9. William Congreve (1670–1729), *The Mourning Bride* (1697) Act I Scene 1: "Music has charms to soothe the savage breast, to soften rocks, or bend a knotted oak."

10. Pierre Teilhard de Chardin, *Hymn of the Universe.*

11. Paul Claudel, *"La Messe La-bas."*

12. Ladislas Örsy, "'Kenosis': The Door to Christian Unity" (talk to NADEO Luncheon 1993) in *Origins* 23 (1993) 38–41. See also Groupe des Dombes, *Pour la Conversion des Eglises: Identité et changement dans la dynamique de communion* (Paris: Centurion, 1992). English trans., *For the Conversion of the Churches* (Geneva: World Council of Churches, 1993).

Bibliography

Anglican Roman Catholic International Commission. *The Final Report.* Washington: United States Catholic Conference, 1982.

Artz, Thomas Robert. *One in the Body of Christ: Robert Isaac Wilberforce and the Theology of Concorporation.* Ann Arbor: University Microfilms International, 1985.

Bernier, Paul. *Ministry in the Church: A Historical and Pastoral Approach.* Mystic, Conn.: Twenty-Third Publications, 1992.

Bieler, L. "Penitentials" in *New Catholic Encyclopedia.* New York: McGraw-Hill, 1967. 11:86–87.

Chenu, M.-D. *Introduction à l'étude de St. Thomas d'Aquin.* Paris: 1950.

Claudel, Paul. *"La Messe Là-bas."*

Congar, Yves. *I Believe in the Holy Spirit.* New York: Seabury, 1983.

Congreve, William. *The Mourning Bride* (1697). Act I, Scene 1.

Conzelmann, Hans. *1 Corinthians: A Commentary on the First Epistle to the Corinthians.* Trans. James W. Leitch, bibliography and reference James W. Kunkly, ed. George W. MacRae. Philadelphia: Fortress Press, 1975.

Cox, Harvey. *The Feast of Fools: A Theological Essay on Festivity and Fantasy.* Cambridge, Mass.: Harvard University Press, 1969.

Crocken, Robert C. *Luther's First Front: The Eucharist as Sacrifice.* Ottawa: University of Ottawa Press, 1990.

Crockett, William R. *Eucharist: Symbol of Transformation,* New York: Pueblo, 1989.

Davies, Horton R. *Bread of Life and Cup of Joy: Newer Ecumenical Perspectives on the Eucharist.* Grand Rapids: Eerdmans, 1993.

Enchiridion Symbolorum, Definitionum et Declarationum de Rebus Fidei et Morum. Ed. Henricus Denzinger/Adolfus Schönmetzer. 36a ed. emedata. Rome: Herder, 1976.

Falardeau, Ernest. *One Bread and Cup: Source of Communion.* Wilmington: Glazier, 1987, Collegeville: The Liturgical Press, 1990.

Gregg, David. *Anamnesis in the Eucharist.* Grove Liturgical Study #5. Bramcotte Notts, England: Grove, 1976.

Groupe des Dombes. *Pour la Conversion des Eglises: Identité et changement dans la dynamique de communion.* Paris: Centurion, 1992. English trans. *For the Conversion of the Churches.* Geneva: World Council of Churches, 1993.

Gutiérrez, Gustavo. *The Theology of Liberation.* Maryknoll, N.Y.: Orbis, 1973.

Kelsey, Morton T. *Dreams: A Way To Listen To God.* New York: Paulist, 1978.

Kidd, B. J. *The Later Medieval Doctrine of the Eucharistic Sacrifice.* London: SPCK (1898) 1958.

Léon-Dufour, Xavier. *Sharing the Eucharistic Bread: The Witness of the New Testament.* Trans. Matthew J. O'Connell. New York: Paulist, 1987.

Lutheran World Federation/Roman Catholic Joint Commission. *Facing Unity: Models, Forms and Phases of Catholic-Lutheran Church Fellowship.* Lutheran World Federation, 1985.

McCue, James F. "Luther and Roman Catholics on the Sacrifice of the Mass," in *Lutherans and Catholics in Dialogue, III: The Eucharist as Sacrifice.* Ed. Paul C. Empie and T. Austin Murphy. Minneapolis: Augsburg, 1965, 45–74.

Marsili, Salvatore. "The Mass, paschal mystery and mystery of the Church" in *The Liturgy of Vatican II: A symposium in two volumes.* Ed. William Barauna. English ed. Jovian Lang. Chicago: Franciscan Herald Press, 1966. 2:4–5.

Nikolasch, Franz. "The Sacrament of Penance: Learning from the East" in *Sacramental Reconciliation.* Ed. Edward Schillebeeckx. Concilium #61. New York: Herder, 1971. 65–75.

Olier, Jean Jacques. *Catéchisme Chrétien.* Paris: Migne, 1856.

Örsy, Ladislas. "'Kenosis': The Door to Christian Unity" (talk to NADEO Luncheon 1993) in *Origins* 23 (1993) 38–41.

Pastor Hermas. Mand. 4, 3, 6. Rouët de Journel. *Enchiridion Patristicum.* 15a ed. Rome: Herder, 1981. #7.

Paul VI. *Revised Roman Missal. Eucharistic Prayer no. 3.*

—————. *Eucharisticum Mysterium.* in *Vatican Council II: The Conciliar and Post Conciliar Documents.* Ed. Austin Flannery, 1981 ed. 100–36.

—————. *Eucharistiae Sacramentum.* in op. cit. 242–53.

Peck, M. Scott. *People of the Lie: the Hope For Healing Human Evil.* New York: Simon and Schuster, 1983.

Pelotte, Donald. *John Courtney Murray Theologian in Conflict.* New York: Paulist, 1975.

Pius XII. *Mediator Dei.* (Encyclical on the Liturgy) Rome: AAS (1947).

Poschmann, B. *Penance and the Anointing of the Sick.* Trans. F. Courtney. New York: 1964.

Power, David N. *The Sacrifice We Offer: The Tridentine Dogma and Its Reinterpretation.* New York: Crossroad, 1987.

Ramos-Regidor, José. "Reconciliation in the Primitive Church and Its Lessons for Theology and Pastoral Practice Today" in *Sacramental Reconciliation.* Ed. Edward Schillebeeckx. Concilium #61. New York: Herder, 1971. 76–88.

Santer, Mark. *The Church's Sacrifice.* Fairacres, Oxford, England: SGL Press, 1975.

Schillebeeckx, Edward. *The Eucharist.* Trans. N. D. Smith. New York: Sheed and Ward, 1968.

Schmemann, Alexander. *The Eucharist: Sacrament of the Kingdom.* Trans. from the Russian by Paul Kachur. Crestwood, N.Y.: St. Vladimir's, 1987.

Sobrino, Jon. "Liberation from Sin" in *Theology Digest* 37 (1990) 141–45.

St. Leo the Great. *Sermo 6 in Nativitate Domini,* 2–5.

Stevenson, Kevin. *Accept This Offering: The Eucharist as Sacrifice Today.* Collegeville: The Liturgical Press, 1989.

Ramsey, Michael. *The Christian Concept of Sacrifice.* Fairacres, Oxford: SLG Press, 1974.

Teilhard de Chardin, Pierre. *The Phenomenon of Man.* New York: Harper and Row, 1959.

_____. *Hymn of the Universe.* New York: Harper and Row, 1965.

_____. *The Divine Milieu.* New York: Harper, 1968, 1960.

Thomas Aquinas. *Summa Theologiae.* II–II, q. 81–100.

Tillard, Jean-Marie-Roger. *The Eucharist: Pasch of God's People.* Staten Island, N.Y.: Alba House, 1966.

_____. "The Bread and Cup of Reconciliation" in *Sacramental Reconciliation.* Ed. Edward Schillebeeckx. Concilium #61. New York: Herder, 1971. 38–54.

Vatican Council II, The Conciliar and Post Conciliar Documents. Ed. Austin Flannery. Northport, N.Y.: Costello, 1975.

Wainwright, Geoffrey. *The Eucharist and Eschatology.* New York: Oxford University Press, 1981.

White, James F. *Sacraments as God's Self Giving: Sacramental Practice and Faith.* Nashville: Abingdon, 1983.

Williams, Rowan. *Eucharistic Sacrifice: The Roots of a Metaphor.* Grove Liturgical Study #31. Bramcote Notts, England: 1982.

Witczak, Michael G. *The Language of Eucharistic Sacrifice:* Immolare *and* Immolatio *in Prefaces of the Roman Tradition.* Thesis ad Lauream #118. Rome: Pontif. Athenaeum Anselmianum, 1987.

World Council of Churches. *Baptism, Eucharist and Ministry.* Faith and Order #111. Geneva: World Council of Churches, 1982.

World Council of Churches. *Toward Koinonia in Faith, Life and Witness.* Faith and Order Conference, Santiago de Compostella (Spain) August 1993. *Ecumenical Trends* 22 (June 1993) 2/82–24/104.